Hoof Physics

How to Recognize the Signs of Hoof Distortion

The Methodology of Preventive Hoof Care
Is a Novel Approach to Solve Hoof Problems
in the Long Term

Nadine Caban

Notices

The information in this book reflects the opinion of the author. They are based on the author's best knowledge and experience but do not relieve the horse owner of their responsibility. They cannot replace professional examination and treatment by a veterinarian or hoof specialist.

Please do not copy any of the hoof trimming techniques shown in this book. Each hoof must be evaluated individually by a professional. With respect to any drug or hoof product identified, readers are advised to consult first with their horse's hoof care practitioner or veterinarian to verify the recommended dose of formula, the method and duration of administration, and contraindications. It is the responsibility of practitioners, relying on their own experience and knowledge of the patient, to make diagnoses, to determine dosages and the best treatment for each individual horse. To the fullest extent of the law, neither the publisher nor the authors, contributors, or editors assume any liability for any injury and or damage to persons or animals as a matter of products liability, negligence or otherwise, or from any use or operation of any methods, products, instructions, or ideas contained in the material herein.

Table of Contents

Acknowledgment

My heartfelt thanks go to all my friends and clients who have actively and morally supported me in this project, especially Brenda Gillespie, Debbie Vreeland and John Caban for their assistance along the way.

I would especially like to thank my German colleagues Angelika Engelmann, Nina Seckel, Anja Küchler and Anke Dänhardt from the German Center for Hoof Orthopedics (www.hufortho.de) who supported me with advice and additional photo material.

About the Author

Nadine Caban is the founder of the Preventive Hoof Care Authority in the United States. Trained at the German Institute for Hoof Orthopedics in Germany, she has been successfully dealing with apparently hopeless cases for over 20 years.

Since 2005 she has educated hundreds of hoof specialists in Germany and now offers training in the United States.

With this book, Nadine guides horse owners to recognize the first signs of hoof deformations, and why hooves deform. Horse owners learn why hoof problems of their horses may not have been solved for a long period of time. Numerous case studies show how prophylaxis can be used to prevent lameness.

Preface

I wrote this book to present an alternative to the existing conventional hoof trimming methods. In 1993, while in Germany, my own horse suffered from hoof problems, and for years, I searched for a solution. I tried every available hoof-trimming approach with little to no success.

Being a farrier's apprentice for a year, I learned how to shoe a horse and later experimented with the first plastic shoes ever developed. I believed that due to the severity of the hoof problems my horse was facing, it would not be possible to find a solution that did not involve using shoes. Even though switching to plastic shoes seemed to make my horse much better, it was not rehabilitated completely. Something was still missing.

During this time, alternative hoof schools were on the rise in Germany, and I experimented extensively with those methodologies as well, yet again, without success. In the end, I was afraid to let my horse walk without permanent hoof protection. I was desperate. The vet's diagnosis was chronic laminitis, and he recommended putting her down. It was only later that I found out, my horse did not have chronic laminitis.

In 1996, I came across a newspaper ad that read, "Are you unhappy with your horse's hooves?"

This would be the ad that would change my life. I contacted the author, Jochen Biernat, the founder of Hoof Orthopedics in Germany.

In ten short minutes, he explained why my horse was limping. The answer was simple and logical. I asked myself, why had I not seen it before?

We tend to rely on traditional values and never question diagnoses or treatments, at least as long as things go well and the outcome is positive, even if it's a minimal improvement or it's only temporary. Sometimes, a change in perspective can illustrate the principle of cause and effect. Suddenly, everything appears clear, and the solution becomes so obvious, it is as if it was always right before your very eyes.

This book is intended to help you recognize the first signs of hoof irregularities and hoof problems in the early stages before your horse is lame, so corrections can be implemented quickly and effectively.

In 1999, I became one of Jochen Biernat's first students. Together, we all established Hoof Orthopedics in Germany and created the Institute for Hoof Orthopedic Treatment. Hoof Orthopedics has been well established in Germany since 1999, and it is an official profession* independent of that of the farrier.

In Germany, the term orthopedics is not reserved for traditional medical practitioners as it is here in the United States. The term was chosen because it simply defines the correction and prevention of malformations and diseases of the musculoskeletal system; the hoof is not only a part but the foundation of that system. That is exactly what the hoof orthopedist does. We treat hooves with simple measures, just by working the hoof horn with hoof knives and a rasp. This is a very specific trimming approach without the use of any affixed aids and 'crutches' for the hoof.

Due to restrictions on the use of terms, I chose the term hoof specialist for my practice in the U.S.

With various schools and over 300 practicing hoof specialists, we cover the necessity for the prevention of hoof distortion in Germany. We work closely with veterinarians, and our approach and knowledge are well accepted. Our 18-month educational curriculum combines medical knowledge with physical implementation, which offers a functional bridge for a holistic approach. Many veterinarians learn our approach alongside their veterinary medical school education. The diagnosis is one thing but knowing and implementing the right approach to healing is quite another.

In 2018, I brought this methodology to the U.S. and have since then helped numerous horses not only achieve healthy hooves but managed to even save some from euthanization.

My goal, moving forward, is to educate as many interested horse owners as possible and create a network of professionals to help the horses in need. My own capacity is limited by the number of owners who are challenged by hoof issues. My goal is to inspire, in others, the same enthusiasm that I possess for utilizing this alternative methodology to achieve healthier hooves. I want to raise awareness of the need for healthy hooves because, in my opinion, most lameness results from hoof conditions that are not physiological. My aim is to provide you the awareness and training you need to accurately read the first signs of hoof distortion.

* In Germany, the profession of the Hoof Orthopedist belongs to the group of professionals who manipulate the hoof for the purpose of protection, health maintenance, correction, or treatment, without applying a metal shoe. The Hoof Orthopedic Center Germany is an institution that trains professionals for this purpose. According to the decision of the Bundesverfassunsgerichtes**, the practice of this profession has been approved since 2007 on the basis of Article 12, Paragraph 1 of the German Constitution.

**The Federal Constitutional Court, which is the equivalent of the United States Supreme Court.

Introduction

In the past 25 years, I have come across many equine hoof experts and their methodologies to correct hooves, most notably in Germany, where there is a greater variety of trimming methods than in the United States. Each and every one of them, somewhat, understandably, suggests he or she has the "right" approach and asserts why their approach is the ultimate solution.

There is one important aspect of each method that remains consistent; that we all strive for the same goal: a healthy hoof.

The notion of what defines healthy, unfortunately, varies among methods. From observations, practitioners appear to be trying to reinvent hoof function continuously instead of accepting the physical relationships within the horses' limbs and understanding the various modes of action inherent in them. The highly intricate anatomical relationships within our horses' limbs are interacting in an ingeniously deliberate construct created by nature itself. Every single part of that construct has a specific function; when each of these functions is combined, the animal is offered full injury prevention through a perfectly designed weight-bearing solution.

I will introduce to you the concept of hoof physics and instruct you on how to better understand and recognize the telltale signs of hoof distortion.

The Ideal Hoof = The Healthy Hoof

What Does the Ideal Hoof Look Like, and Who Determines What Is "Ideal"?

The answer to that question is quite simple, the horse itself! We, as professionals, cannot assume that rasping the hoof into an ideal shape of our own choosing creates an ideal hoof. It is desirable, of course, to achieve perfectly aligned hoof-pastern axis and mediolateral (inside to outside) symmetry, but ultimately, previously deformed internal structures of the limb dictate how the hoof capsule inevitably will shape, and every single hoof is unique.

Repeatedly, attempts are made to abruptly change the statics of the hoof capsule with the belief that this also will immediately alter the horse's hoof usage or even out the load on that hoof. Unfortunately, this is not possible for horses. Horses are unguligrade animals with hinge joints and therefore cannot adapt to abrupt changes in hoof positions; this will be explained in this book.

The Preventive Hoof Care Methodology is a completely different approach, unlike any other hoof trimming method known so far.

The Preventive Hoof Care approach is the most non-invasive, gentle hoof correction known. The science behind this approach has been developed over a period of 35 years in Germany and is now a well-established and widely utilized practice across Europe.

Hoof specialists have thousands of case studies that demonstrate rehabilitative hoof progress; each case is individually documented to confirm the improvement of every single hoof treated in this manner.

But what is so significant about gentle?

Employing a non-invasive approach to treating the hoof eliminates any abrupt change in the position of a horse's limb.

All other existing hoof-trimming methods have one thing in common:

They all correct a hoof shape by cutting, rasping or nipping parts of the hoof wall unevenly in order to create the ideal hoof, which forces the horse to use or load its limb differently.

This can become incredibly problematic for a horse's joints and affect its health in the long run. We will explore this in depth in the first chapter.

What if the horse itself could decide when and how fast the correction takes place by 'walking itself into physiological shape' gradually and pain-free so that the internal structures can get used to the new situation?

It would be an effective long-term solution for hoof deformities, prevention of hoof problems, and healing of the actual cause of a hoof distortion instead of just putting a Band-Aid over the symptom. The hoof heals itself with just a little help from science.

With applied physics from the Preventive Hoof Care Authority, we can make it happen!

We must assist a little bit because we breed our pet horses in order to ride them. We removed them from their natural habitat. We created different and non-natural living conditions for them. Hence, comparing our pet animal hooves with those of wild horses as an ideal is not a practical approach.

Although wild horses actually deal with similar hoof problems, due to natural selection, only the strongest and the healthiest survived and kept on breeding with good hoof conditions. They are not being ridden. They don't get Fast Food. They are able to move all day instead of standing bored in a stall. We are simply unable to provide such ideal living conditions for our pet horses. So, aiming to create a hoof that looks similar to that of a wild-living horse is not suitable for our horses.

The theory that wild horses all show ground parallelism of their coffin bone has long been disproved by various scientists. The hooves of our wild horses, no matter where on this planet, are as different as their individual hoof problems. Their varied living conditions determine how the horse is forced to use its feet and hence how the individual hoof will be shaped.

A Mustang hoof from the Rockies will naturally be more worn and shorter, with a rounded hoof wall, as Mustangs run on hard stony ground and dig for water.

The Camargue Horses, tough, brave ponies living wild in the wetlands of the southeast of France, live in wet, soft, swampy surfaces. Their hooves adapt to that and flare terribly. They are flat and wide due to the bent hoof walls. They have little to no abrasion, and their hooves adapted to those living conditions over thousands of years.

They are exposed to the same physical forces that deform their hooves as our pet horses.

Hooves always adapt to the surrounding conditions in which they are used and how they are used.

We need to make them suitable for those individual living conditions. Keeping the hooves healthy means treating them individually and arrange the living conditions suited to their individual needs.

Taking one single hoof model as our ideal is not only wrong, it will inevitably harm our horses.

This book will teach how to recognize individual deformations, which differ in every single hoof.

Recognizing signs of distortion and how to reverse them requires a thorough education with long-term training and cannot be learned by simply taking an internet course!

The Methodology of Preventive Hoof Care

The aim of this methodology is to achieve a physiological balance between the external hoof capsule and the internal structures suspended within it, in particular the coffin bone. In order to form the hoof back into its best possible physiological shape, the hoof specialist makes use of the same physical forces that have deformed the hoof.

Firstly, one must be able to read those physical forces that form and deform a hoof and understand what is happening inside the hoof capsule itself. The hoof specialist must thoroughly learn to recognize and evaluate the signs of deformation for each individual hoof. There is no general scheme, no map, and no measuring, just simple physics. Once you understand the real cause of these signs and the causal chain that led to the symptoms and, even further, to the deformity, you are able to treat the real cause by eliminating the deforming factors and allow the hoof to grow back into its physiological shape. Simple, right?

The only work material necessary to restore a hoof is the constantly renewing hoof horn itself.

Instead of manually shortening the hoof wall abruptly, and one-sided, the hoof specialist files certain individual parts of the hoof wall from the outside using a special and unique filing technique. This technique is called the Thatched Roof Technique. The technique as such will not be explained further in this book, only its results are shown. It is an integral part of our comprehensive 1.5 year education program.

With this technique, the abrasion of the hoof horn is manipulated, meaning it can be determined how much and where exactly the horse will have wear on the hoof in the next few weeks. This precision technique eliminates leverage, which a lot of barefoot trimmers already found out to be necessary to address. It also controls the amount of wear and location of wear on the hoof capsule in the future. It gives the horse the opportunity to walk itself into the needed shape.

It is essential to eliminate all disturbing factors that in the past made it uncomfortable for the horse to use its hoof completely, or more precisely, to wear out certain parts of the hoof wall.

"My horse is walking funny." Or "Look, how he is standing." These are phrases that the hoof specialist hears again and again.

The horse CAN'T stand or walk any other way because interfering hoof wall parts are in the way during the movement. The horse has developed a compensatory movement pattern to avoid uncomfortable or even painful positions. Hoof wall parts can hurt because they have become longer than other wall parts due to the lack of abrasion. The excessive hoof wall length generates leverage which is very uncomfortable for the horse to stand on. Hoof wall parts that are too long can start to bend, causing the tubular horn to deviate from the coffin bone. Tensile forces pull the hoof wall away from its inner structure. Accumulated hoof wall length can also cause compression. The hoof wall tubules can fold in wrinkles. The reason for this to happen is simply because the weight of the horse is pushing against the ground, while the hoof in between is exposed to the physical forces working against each other.

Just to give an example, the hoof wall horn accumulates, starts to cause compression into the coronet, or causes leverage, and the horn tubules start to bend, flare, crack, or chip and any combination thereof. All these symptoms show that the hoof is not equally loaded and can lead to lameness! Some parts experience more load. Other parts are being pushed, distracted, and pulled away from that center of load. If not corrected, the inner bone structures will respond and adapt to the load imbalance with bone alterations. Once the bone and joint deformation continue, the hoof capsule, in turn, will now try to adapt to that new ongoing situation, and a vicious cycle begins.

How Can the Manipulation of Abrasion Restore a Hoof Shape?

The technique utilized by Preventive Hoof Care interrupts this vicious cycle. It transforms disturbing negative physical forces into positive forces. Disturbing 'obstacles' (accumulated horn) over which the horse had to break over before do not disturb anymore. The horse begins to use its hoof, the entire limb differently, more comfortably. As a result, parts of the hoof wall that did not have any abrasion before are being worn and used now. The horse is the one that decides how quickly it is able to use the hoof differently. It is given the opportunity but is not forced. The limb has time to get used to the new situation. A 'letting become' instead of a repetitive 'cutting into' an ideal hoof image chosen by us.

The horse is not being forced into anything. If it is not able to use its limb differently due to predispositions or defects it will not be abruptly forced to use its hoof differently. The hoof will then stay in the shape the inner structures determine. That doesn't mean that conditions cannot be improved to the maximum possible extent. Ongoing deforming factors can at least always be slowed down and mitigated. By eliminating leverage and changing dynamics within the horn tubules of the hoof wall, the coronary band which produces the hoof wall receives different stimuli. Without tensile and compressive forces that would change the angulation of the newly produced horn, the tubules of the hoof wall can now grow down unhindered, parallel to the coffin bone. It will now be balanced to the inner hoof, which actually gives the physiological shape. That is the ideal hoof as nature has constructed it.

Let's talk hoof physics...

Chapter 1:

What Forms and Deforms a Hoof

Is a Horse Born with Sloping Hooves?

Very often during my career I have heard from other trimmers the explanation for hoof deformities that the horse was already born with its crooked hooves. This statement can be true in some cases – some horses are born with genetic anomalies and predispositions, but mainly hooves acquire their maldevelopment later, postnatally, and I want to focus on those later acquired deformities in this book.

The foal is born, and immediately after birth, it stands on its own legs. For the first time, the weight of the foal works against ground reacting forces. According to very simple laws of physics, all horn parts of the hoof (such as hoof wall, frog, sole, and bars) that are not directly located underneath the main load will take the path of least resistance and deform away from the center of pressure. This center rarely tends to be the middle of the hoof. It is where the peak load is concentrated.

Especially the foal, due to its disproportionate length ratio between its short neck and long legs, must very often shift the load between the front legs to reach the ground. It will favor one foot before the other. Very soon, in the early days, hoof horns, hoof wall horn, sole horn, bulbs, bars and frog all start to adapt accordingly to the load. Gradually, they start to deform in a certain direction. The joints, bones, ligaments, and tendons, in particular, begin to develop accordingly.

Already in the first days the articular surfaces of the hinge joints will be loaded unilaterally or at least unevenly. The way to the medio-lateral imbalance is paved. Later the newly reproduced horn tubules of the hoof wall will always try to grow down, following the existing inner imbalances, due to their close connection to the bones, mainly the coffin bone.

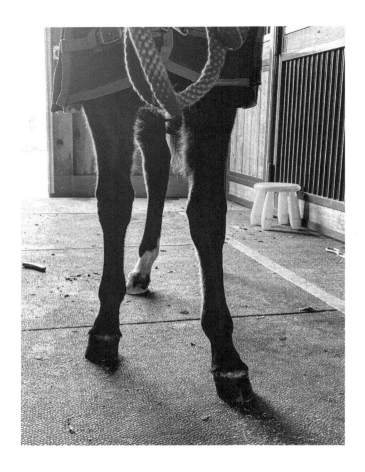

10-month-old foal, already dealing with imbalanced limbs

If the correct hoof treatment were given to the foal early enough, later anomalies could be prevented. But what foal is lucky enough to receive correction in the first two weeks? And what kind of correction does it receive?

Very soon the foal will favor one foot, and tendons will be stressed differently, especially the Deep Digital Flexor Tendon (DDFT), whose main function is to flex the coffin bone in the coffin joint. Under strain, it reliably prevents the coffin bone from rotating in its hoof capsule. It is therefore crucial how the horse loads its limbs.

Different tendon growth stimuli lead to different tendon lengths. These different growth stimuli in the early age of a horse, along with the relationship between bone and tendon length, are therefore significantly involved in how the individual hoof-pastern axis will be angled. In addition, there are influencing factors involved, such as living conditions, feeding and genetic predispositions of the horse.

(See section – Club Foot/Laminitis)

Suspensory Apparatus of the Hoof

The coffin bone as the furthest distal phalanx is suspended in the inner hoof wall through the connection of dermal lamellae and epidermal lamellae of the inner hoof wall. This very strong relationship of dermis and renewing horn product offers a protective construct for the coffin bone suspended in a strong hoof wall, functioning as the main weight bearer (weight bearing foundation).

The load of the bone column is transferred to the bearing edge of the hoof wall via the suspensory apparatus. Conversely, a functional hoof wall protects the limb from concussions and deforming forces as the main foundation on which the horse stands. I just stated the term functional because if the foundation is unable to withstand the forces, the bone column will inevitably deform in the later stages.

The Dilemma of What We Wish to Have the Hoof Look Like vs. What It Actually Ends Up Looking Like

Dorsal view of a right fore-foot

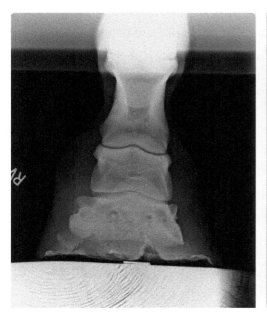
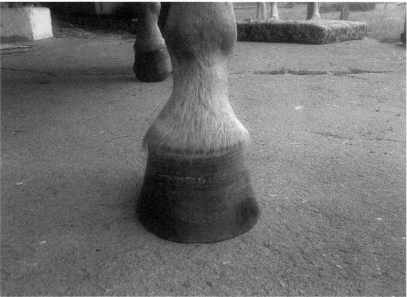

The x-ray of that foot clearly shows the non-symmetrical bone column and how the one-sided load (in the picture to the right) has shaped the articular surfaces of the joints. The long thin proximal phalanx (P1) is straighter under the load on the right side, leaving a deeper and pointier groove in the articular fovea of the pastern joint. The same happens with the middle phalanx similarly in its coffin joint, being more compressed on the more loaded side. The whole group straightens out under the main load. That hoof has less sole depth on that side as well, meaning that the coffin bone is closer to the ground than on the other side. The left half of that column is 'moving away' from that load and begins to form wider, especially the coffin bone can now assume an unsymmetrical shape. The bones and their joints remodel (deform).

In the hoof photo, we see the adapted hoof capsule alteration. Although covered with skin and hair, we can still see the deformation of the proximal phalanx.

The hoof tries to follow accordingly. It seems wider on the left side (blue curve). From the x-ray, we now know what is responsible for that. We see signs of compression on the right side of the picture in the hoof wall near the coronary band. The forces work proximally (upward) into the coronet. The coronet has no other choice but to be pushed upward. Accumulated horn tubule length (hoof wall length) works as a leverage into the coronet. Due to the load situation, the jammed horn cannot 'flee' outward to the side as it can do on the lateral hoof wall (left in the picture). The horizontal 'wrinkles' are closer to each other on the right side, more compressed. While forces can go outward on the left side, they work upward on the right, which is the more loaded side.

Simple physics!

The trained eye will be able to know how the bone column, especially the coffin bone is already deformed asymmetrically, without any need for x-ray. This requires comprehensive training and experience that cannot be found in any book or online course. If this horse would live in the wilderness and would have constant horn abrasion, it could keep its hoof wall short. While it would minimize deforming factors, the horse will not be able to eliminate them. The hoof would still deform, since it is not only leverage that deforms a hoof.

Let's have a closer look at further deforming factors and their consequences on the statics of the limb and its biomechanics. The arrows in the picture indicate how that hoof is exposed to different mechanical forces acting against each other. Eventually, the hoof capsule here will deform.

The red line indicates the natural abraded part of the front hoof

Every front hoof has a natural abraded toe, meaning the part where the horse wears its toe wall the most naturally when pushing the hoof off the ground. Only the front hooves should show that abraded part in the toe because the hind limb of a horse has different biomechanics than the front limb.

While the horse pushes itself off the ground in the front during locomotion, it rather lifts its hind feet due to a special mechanism, an interaction of muscles and tendons, the so-called reciprocal apparatus. Stifle and hock are synchronized in their direction of movement, i.e., a flexion of the stifle always results in a flexion of the hock.

This leads to a lifting of the limb compared to a 'pushing' off or breaking over in the front foot, and gives the hind feet a rather oval form compared to a round form in the front feet. Therefore, there may be no visible sign of abrasion in the toe of a hind foot. If there is, then the horse will probably have a problem lifting its hind limb.

The main deformation of a horse's limb happens during peak load in the stance phase. That developed shape will influence the usage and shape of all four limbs throughout the life of a horse.

Another important forming factor, mainly for the front feet, is the lift-off phase when the horse pushes its hoof off the ground in forward locomotion.

The abraded part of that hoof is always located in the toe wall and is only there due to the stiffness of the hinge joints and their inability to tilt. It is the part where the hoof has the most abrasion naturally. Of course, there are other parts of the hoof that have abrasion, according to one-sided load and distortion. We will get to those later.

The abraded toe can occur in the middle of the toe or offset from, more medial or lateral, depending on how the hoof has shaped in the past due to usage.

Three different right forefeet with different locations of the abraded toe are given below:

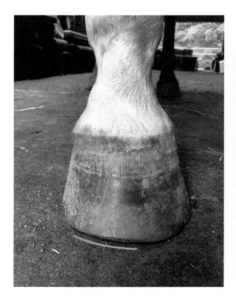
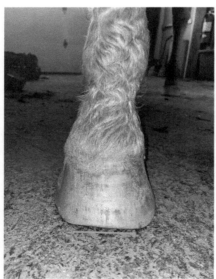

No matter where the abraded toe is located, the accumulated, non-abraded horn left and right from it makes it uncomfortable for the horse and nearly impossible to break over. That leads to a forced directional usage of the hoof that will deform the whole hoof even more in the future if not corrected.

The Longer the General Hoof Wall Length, the Greater the Effect of Leverage

The bearing edge, which is the rim of the hoof wall that touches the ground, should be the main weight bearer. The longer that rim is, the more mechanical forces have a chance to distort it. Many trimmers therefore believe that the sole should bear the main load and the bearing edge should be eliminated for this reason.

Unfortunately, it is not that easy. Even a hoof with very little or no bearing edge length is still exposed to the physical effects.

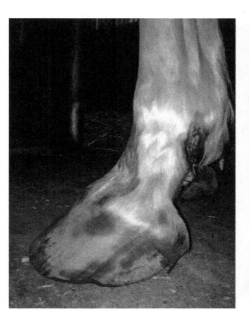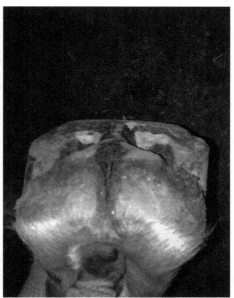

Here you can see the hoof wall was regularly filed off from below and the sole was brought to bear the main weight. The hoof-pastern axis is broken back, the heels – what is left of them – underrun and contracted. There is no bearing edge left that the horse could walk on. Sole and frog bear the entire weight. The bars are on the same level as the sole. Due to this situation, the toe wall, if not corrected, will make it hard for the horse to break over. Although there is no hoof wall length to shorten, the toe wall creates a huge lever that forces the weight more to the back of the hoof. The mechanics of the underrun heel work against the stiff quarter and the toe wall. The hoof wall cracks exactly where those different mechanics collide.

The entire levering toe wall forces the hoof backward and is an obstacle in the horse's motion. It is like having to walk in clown shoes for a human.

I often hear the phrase from other 'professionals':

"The horse's toe is too long! That's why he is so flat. The toe needs to be cut more!"

This is not true, for the toe is not too long. It is just incorrectly angled. There is no excessive hoof wall length. The horse is already walking on its sole. What exactly is there to cut off?

The right method would be filing the hoof in a way that the horse feels more comfortable breaking over that toe wall. In the pictures of the previous page, the horn tubules of the toe wall were being robbed of their function, the rim eliminated but the problem not solved.

Allowing the sole to do the main weight bearing work poses another problem. The solar dermis is a modified periosteum. The sole is a sensitive tensile organ, not very thick and certainly not meant to bear the main load. *The rim of the hoof wall where the horse is standing on is called the 'bearing edge' for a reason.*

A lot of horses are very 'ouchy' or sore on hard surfaces because they are missing a proper bearing edge to walk on. In the course of the right treatment, they will become lesser and lesser sensitive to the point where they will need no hoof protection at all when being ridden since the sole is protected again. Here too, our domesticated horse cannot be compared with the wild living horse that is not being ridden. The individual hoof shape and how much abrasion the hooves are exposed to determine the thickness of the sole. A sole that is too thin can be as uncomfortable as a sole that has been left to thicken under piled up exfoliated horn layers that cause pressure. The hoof specialist therefore uses a hoof tester and experience in order to determine the correct sole thickness for the individual hoof.

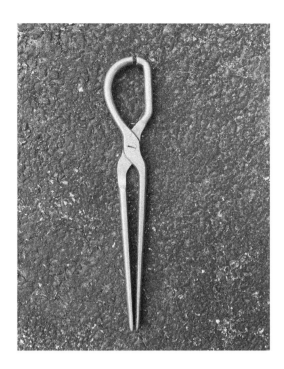

Hoof tester, an indispensable tool to determine the thickness and sensitivity of the sole

The hoof wall is a powerful protective barrier connected by the lamellae with the coffin bone. It is the major weight bearer and is exposed the most to all the physical forces. That's why it is so important to create a statically strong construct as a foundation on which the horse stands, an equally loaded foundation.

A friend of mine, an architect, described it in his own words:

> *"When one wall of a house is overloaded, it can crack, and if this one wall collapses, the whole house collapses."*

The Problem of Conventional Hoof Trimming or One-Sided Hoof Shortening

Deformities of the hooves are so problematic because the horse's weight rests on a relatively thin column of bones suspended in tendons, ligaments and tissue and on the distal bones of this column in their single foundation, the hoof capsule. All tension, pressure and tensile forces (pulling forces) are transmitted to the bone column via the hoof capsule, or more precisely, through the supporting rim and lamellae. The joints of this column consist of hinge joints, so the horse is not able to tilt to the side. This is in direct contrast to humans who can bend their ball joint in the foot to avoid unevenness. The unshod hoof capsule can adapt to unevenness due to its ability to twist, but it cannot tip over to the side completely.

For example, take any finger and press it straight down, vertically, on a hard surface. You will feel compression in each joint of that finger; maybe the pressure continues into the wrist as well. Try to tilt the finger to the side using only the end joint. It won't work. Depending on the length of your fingernail, the position of the contact surface of the fingertip will also vary. If the nail is too long, it will not be possible to place the finger vertically on the surface. In fact, you will immediately feel unpleasant shear forces in the nail bed because the nail is being pulled away from its connective tissue (tensile forces). Fortunately, we as humans can determine how much pressure we ought to apply to the finger, but what about the horse that is forced to stand on its fingernail? In addition, our nail has a beautiful convex shape when viewed from the side because it does not experience any counter-pressure at all. The horse has permanent counter-pressure from the ground it is permanently standing or walking on. For this reason, the hooves deform. *All impact, compression and tensile forces are transferred to the inflexible hinge joints, which over time have already assumed a certain asymmetry depending on the individual load situation.*

After a few years, the hoof capsule has adapted accordingly and follows this requirement for the joints of the entire bone column. As a result, certain parts of the hoof wall are less stressed, have less wear and abrasion, and may have become longer over the years than other parts of the hoof wall because they are used and worn off more accordingly. They may also be crooked or bent. If these longer wall parts are simply shortened in order to cut this hoof to make it 'look nice' or to achieve an ideal medio-lateral balance optically, the horse will develop a problem during the course of this kind of trimming.

Between each trimming interval, the horse desperately tries to mold the shape to the already existing bone and joint deformations. The hoof trimmer then abruptly changes that situation with every trim by shortening the hoof one-sided and 'balancing' out uneven length. In the long run, undesirable deformations are not corrected at all. In fact, the contrary happens.

Between the trimming intervals, the horse will try to compensate for the lack of hoof wall length with compensatory postures, e.g., to twist the hoof, turn it in, turn it out, etc., to walk 'weird until the missing length has grown back exactly as before... just so the trimmer can cut it off again. And again. And again.

The bones, especially the coffin bone, will not follow a desired ideal abrupt correction by cutting the hoof capsule into shape. They can't. The hoof walls will inevitably move further away from the inner center instead of being balanced.

I often hear, "Well, we do the correction slowly, little by little, so the joints can get used to it. The horse never complains."

Yes, it does, by deforming its bones more, little by little. Even the slightest one-sided height adjustment is still abrupt. Some horses might not complain immediately, and not in English. For many horses even a millimeter is too much, considering how narrow a joint space is. The horse will complain through its body language, doing so by compensating for the uncomfortable feeling with a change of posture or gait pattern.

We have to do exactly the opposite. We have to accept the given, inner bone shape and adapt the outer horn shoe to it and make it comfortable. With this approach, we enable the horse to lead a functionally pain-free life and to make it usable for our purposes. We owe that to the horse.

It Doesn't Matter Whether the Hoof Is 'Beautiful', It Must Be Healthy

Fortunately, with the right treatment, both can be achieved at the same time. The negative results of one-sided shortening can clearly be seen in the following picture.

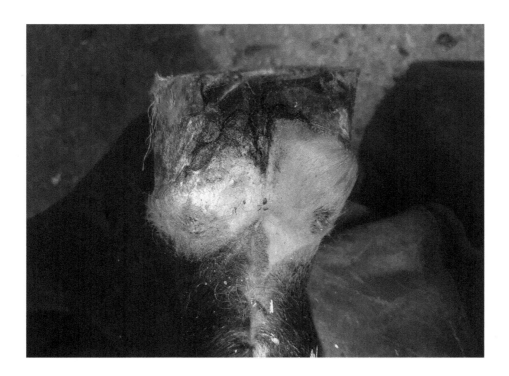

Over the years the hoof had been systematically shortened on the slanting, originally longer hoof wall (right side in the picture) repeatedly in order to achieve a plane landing. The theory of plane landing is a widely held doctrine in most hoof trimming approaches. The hoof is loaded mainly on the left side. The quarter wall on that side is straight. It stands under the weight. The opposite hoof wall started bending, being pushed away from the main load. The hoof wall on that side became slanted. In order to adjust height, the longer-appearing crooked side was cut off. However, the slant of the quarter wall was not corrected, as this is not possible with cutting from below.

In the course of time, this slanting and now much shorter quarter wall has lost ground height (distance from the coronet to the ground). It has sunk. You can clearly see how the bulbs in the rear area have already shifted.

An attempt was made to ensure that the hoof touches the ground, heel first, with all parts of the hoof wall being even when walking to achieve an even load of the hoof. The landing is thus equated with the load. *But this is by no means the case.*

The limb experiences the main load in the stance phase, in mid-stance when the limb is completely under the weight of the horse and thus deforms, not the short moment when the foot is landing.

It can therefore be that the horse touches the ground with the part of the hoof that has become longer (longer because less worn down due to less abrasion) or with the more loaded, shorter side first. If a horse already has severe bone deformations and the hoof is accordingly asymmetrical, it might not be able to land evenly! So, it can be that the already more used side is cut even shorter or the less used, longer side. This measure will result in damaging compressive loads on the joint surfaces and tensile loading on the adjacent ligaments.

An Even Hoof Loading Cannot Be Achieved Through Manipulation of the Landing Behavior

The medio-lateral balance – the symmetry of the bone column when viewed dorsally – cannot be achieved by one-sided hoof wall shortening. A sloping, unloaded side will not straighten if you cut it off from below. It does become shorter but not straight.

The leverage caused by the concavely bent hoof wall tubules is still in the hoof wall and continues to transfer negative dynamics into the coronet.

Hooves are being shortened only on one side in order to achieve a reloading of the limb. However, the horse cannot completely change the load of the limb due to the existing deformation of the stiff hinge joints and their inability to tilt.

The correct way is to achieve a change in the usage of the hoof in a way that the horse is within its capabilities to gauge.

Which suggests the correct way is to control the abrasion. Hoof wall length and orientation will be corrected only on those parts that require correction: individually and never schematically. How much and where the abrasion takes place on the hoof must be determined. *The horse itself makes the shortening of the material happen* by walking itself into the correct shape. The long-term goal is not to let the hoof lose its shape first, but to keep it. Logically, this only works with the barefoot. But then how is it with a shod horse? *The shaping factors are ground reacting forces and abrasion.* The continuously reproduced horn grows down towards the ground and is worn off there on contact. But what happens when the hoof is provided with permanent hoof protection, such as a metal shoe or plastic shoe, glued or nailed? The hoof as a result experiences no natural abrasion.

The Dilemma of the Shod Hoof

With the domestication of the horse and its use as a means of transport, a solution for the increased horn abrasion had to be found very soon. The horse used to be a farm animal, used for carrying loads in the cavalry or pulling the cart. The ancient Romans developed the first metal variants of hoof protection, initially used to strap them to the hoof and later nailed. Alternatives made of leather were also tried.

Nowadays, the horse is mainly bred to fulfill our selfish interests or hobbies. It is no longer a necessity in our lives, thanks to vehicles. The horse is no longer used to any extent as it was originally centuries ago, but the use of metal shoes has not decreased. Metal shoes are still often used, even for horses that are only worked one hour a day and otherwise spend their time on relatively soft turnouts or in the stable. One wonders why the metal shoe is still needed at all. Its original function, a simple abrasion protection and nothing else, is misused in the context of tradition as a means to correct misalignments. As previously described, 'shortening the hoof into shape' is counterproductive in the long run.

However, with the use of a metal shoe, the hoof trimmer has no choice but to prepare the hoof for the shoe by cutting off parts. In addition, the hoof wears disproportionately on the shoe in the heel area. A lack of abrasion and accumulation of the horn length leads to an intensification of the leverage forces. Also, the trimming intervals with the shoe are often far too long, sometimes twice as long. The hoof should, in actuality, be corrected in short intervals to prevent deformation. A good farrier is often chosen based on how long the shoe will stay on the hoof.

However, due to the rigidity of the metal shoe, the hoof capsule is severely impaired in its functionality. It is not possible to cling to the ground and twist the hoof capsule to compensate for unevenness.

The hoof does not only widen when it lands, as is shown in the explanation of the hoof mechanism. This is overly simplistic 2-dimensional thinking. If this were the case, the blood circulation in the hoof on the metal shoe would not be impaired.

However, the hoof is exposed to various mechanics, which do not recur to the same extent as it happens in fixed mechanisms but arbitrarily, depending on the individual hoof shape, in all dimensions, not just in width. Therefore, I'd rather use the word hoof mechanics because each individual hoof is exposed to different mechanical randomly occurring forces. Those mechanics are limited by the use of a metal shoe.

Due to the rigidity of metal, the joints are exposed to sudden shock. Furthermore, the horse is deprived of its sense of touch. An unshod horse feels through its hoof; stimuli are transmitted to the corium. The horse feels the slightest of unevenness, hard, stony, painful ground conditions under its hooves. It adjusts as it walks accordingly. A horse without a sense of touch will not spare its legs. The metal shoe acts like a painkiller.

What Determines the Correct Heel Height?

In the opinion of supporters of the metal shoe, the device serves not only as abrasion protection but also to keep the limbs healthy and correct in shape. One very popular use of the horseshoe is to correct a hoof-pastern axis that is broken back. According to the textbook, the ideal is the unbroken line connecting the joints of the three distal phalanges.

Aligned	Broken back (hyperextended)	Broken forward

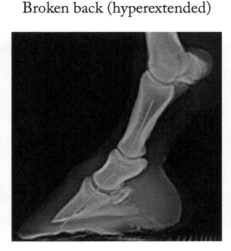 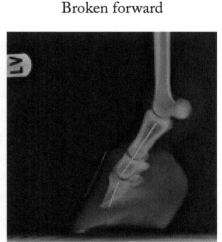

Unfortunately, not every horse is born with this perfect situation. Later in adulthood, the horse has already grown accustomed to acquired anomalies. The tendons, mainly the *Deep Digital Flexor Tendon (DDFT) and the extensor tendons, which hold the distal phalanges in position are the decisive factors that determine the hoof-pastern axis. This axis and how the coffin bone is suspended in its hoof capsule determine the physiological heel height for every hoof individually.*

It is usually not possible for the horse to adapt its hoof-pastern axis to an ideal human-desired image. As already explained, the joint surfaces as well as the horse's entire body have already been set up for precisely this individual situation.

A horse with a flexion in the coffin joint (x-ray broken forward) will need more heel height than a horse with a flat bone axis.

However, it is mandatory to align the hoof capsule to its individual coffin bone. The hoof is considered healthy if its coffin bone is uniformly suspended in its hoof capsule. This can be achieved by eliminating any deformation forces that will distract the horn shoe from its inner bone, which is shown in the 3rd x-ray with the flexed coffin bone. The toe is deflected from its coffin bone, not parallelly suspended in it. When the hoof capsule is deformed, the bone is no longer evenly suspended in its foundation. The lamellae that connect the hoof wall to the bone are inevitably stretched, elongated, which can be seen from the solar view. The hoof wall then shows bending, compression, signs of deformation.

X-ray No 2 of the broken back hoof-pastern axis shows parallelism of hoof wall and bone only in the toe, but you can see the underrun heels. The horn tubules of the heel are not parallel to the horn tubules of the toe wall. Such a hoof cannot be evenly loaded. The heels have more load and the heel wall collapses. For this reason, the hoof-pastern axis is broken backward. The goal is a stable orientation of the horn tubules to the ground, a slight convexity of the hoof wall exactly as the inner bone is shaped, and also parallelism of the horn tubules of the heel with those of correctly oriented toe wall tubules. This ratio characterizes the individual and healthy heel height of the hoof, no matter which hoof-pastern axis the horse was given by nature.

The correct physiological thickness of the sole cannot be measured or determined by some universal standard. The sole depth needs to be assessed individually for each hoof. Factors such as living conditions and usage of the horse influence the abrasion of hoof horn and need to be considered.

It is therefore important that the hoof specialist recognizes if the hoof situation is physiological or if certain deformations have altered the location of the coffin bone in the horn shoe.

The before and after pictures below show a horse with a broken back axis. With the correct heel length, the situation can be improved if the situation before was unphysiological, meaning the heels were collapsed.

11 months later:

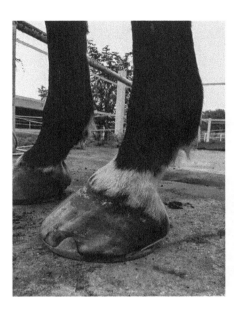 

Once the best possible adjustment is reached, it will be impossible to improve the situation any further:

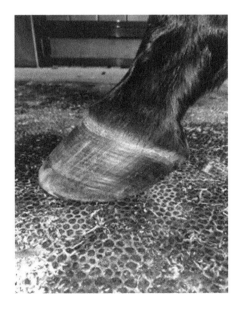

The heels are aligned with the toe but the toe-pastern axis is still broken back. This is the physiological situation for the limb above and needs to be accepted.

The balance between internal and external structure cannot be achieved by mechanically altering the hoof-pastern axis through externally applied devices such as a shoe. If the hoof is too flat with flat angled heel horn tubules, they will still remain incorrectly angled on the shoe. The problem would only be covered up; the heel will remain unstable. The statics of the hoof is being compromised, resulting in an ever-increasing deviation from internal and external structures. Physiological turns into unphysiological. This causes the entire limb to lose its balance. It is more logical to improve the shape of the hoof capsule, to give it the chance to grow a stable foundation to bear weight.

If we want to improve the hoof-pastern axis, we need to let the heels grow in a different orientation to become more stable. Collapsed heels will recover as soon as the whole hoof is rasped the correct way, especially the toe, which is often taken out of function. Only then will functioning hoof mechanics with unhindered blood circulation be guaranteed.

Nevertheless, there is a desire to 'lift up' hooves mechanically that are too flat with the help of a shoe.

The ends of the shoe are often raised with wedges to align the hoof-pastern axis. With this measure, however, the heels are abruptly compressed and cause a sudden change in statics for which the narrow joint surfaces often cannot compensate. In the long term, this measure is even counterproductive.

An abrupt and artificial uplift in the heel area creates pressure. Pressure on the heel creates increased abrasion, which still takes place on the metal shoe in the heel area. The following picture shows the signs of wear for both, horn and metal. Deep traces of wear are left behind on the metal.

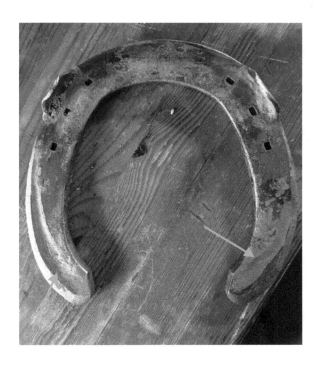

The horn tubules of the heel wall will lose their alignment over time due to the increased pressure, and will be pushed under even further. The strong stiff toe wall, however, no longer experiences abrasion and grows out unhindered in a forward direction. Even setting the shoe back to achieve a better break-over point in the toe does not help the entire statics of the hoof. The horse cannot abrade the toe wall better because the entire toe wall is already too flat in angulation, and the heel has lost its support function. This will force the hoof further back. A vicious cycle begins. The heels become flatter while the toe wall is completely deprived of its carrying function and both the quarter and heel wall become overloaded.

The horse will find it increasingly difficult to break over the toe and all of the weight will progressively shift backward from where the problem will eventually get worse.

The overall known side effects of the horseshoe are known and have previously been discussed in various hoof textbooks of the past. I would like to focus on the effects of permanent protection on the hoof capsule.

A plastic shoe will not help correct a hoof problem either. Although plastic shoes do not have the same negative side effects that the metal ones do; They are not rigid, are lighter than the traditional metal shoe, and allow for the possibility of the hoof capsule to naturally twist.

However, they come with their own negative side effects. One major factor is particularly problematic: the absence of natural wear on the hoof.

Without abrasion, every hoof will inevitably deform faster. While every hoof deforms without proper treatment, it will deform even faster if the natural abrasion is withheld. If the abrasion is greater than the amount of regrowing horn, the animal naturally needs hoof protection when it is used.

Because of this, effective compromises have been developed over the last few years that are only temporarily attached to the hoof, namely when the horse is also being used (hoof boots). A healthy hoof is able to maintain perfect balance, even on the very abrasive floors without any protection.

Most of my customers who initially needed permanent hoof protection never got to need hoof protection again after the hoof was rehabilitated, even in abrasive living conditions.

Chapter 2:

Recognizing Signs of Deformation and the Approach of Preventive Hoof Care

The case studies in this book represent only small excerpts from the daily work of a hoof specialist.

The few examples listed in this book are only intended to touch on a few specific topics. They do not by any means encompass the overall extent and the healing potential that this methodology offers.

Although I show after-treatment pictures, I do not endorse imitating the filing technique without proper training. It is a highly manipulative tool which, when used without sufficient training, can also influence the hoof into the wrong direction and do harm.

Therefore, I will not show in any book or clinic exactly how this technique works because this is part of a 1.5 year well-established and comprehensive education. Working with horses' hooves should be reserved for specialists with a proper education. I repeat that it cannot be learned via an online course or clinics and requires much experience in the field.

Example 1

This is a left front hoof, dorsal view.

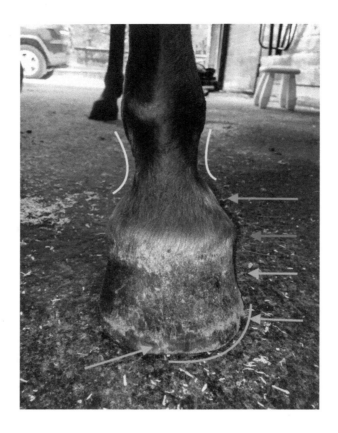

Here we have what appears to be at a first glance, a relatively normal-looking hoof. The medial and lateral hoof walls are shaped differently. Particular attention is directed to the coronary band. It is not balanced. On the right side of the picture, on the lateral side, it shows a greater coronet-ground distance (blue arrow). The coronet seems to be pushed upwards. The drawn-in arches (yellow) illustrate the different deformation of the long pastern bone and thus also the uneven shape of the short pastern bone (red arrow). Over the years, the limb has adapted and deformed to a corresponding load situation. The medial hoof wall (left) appears straighter and more elongated while the lateral hoof wall (in the picture on the right) is clearly bent.

The naturally abraded toe is relatively centered. But why is the coronet not even?

Let's have a look at the bearing edge, the section of the hoof wall that touches the ground.

The green curved line indicates the area where the hoof wall seems to have an *unphysiological rounding* with a toe crack at the end of it. The green arrow show exactly the part of the toe wall that flares the most.

That flare creates a lever, an obstacle for the horse which makes it impossible for the horse to use its hoof and walk over. Due to the lack of use/abrasion, the hoof has the most horn tubule length at this point. Since the horn tubules cannot wear off, they have no choice but to bend. This creates tensile forces in the lower part of the hoof wall, below the bending point (green arrow) and at the same time a strong leverage into the coronet (blue arrow).

The horn that connects the hoof wall and skin is being pushed upward due to the compression the lever causes.

The leverage effect of that hoof wall section (the pulling to the side) collides with the section that is abraded in the toe. Unequal mechanics act in opposite directions. The abraded toe is subjected to compressive forces acting proximally (upward) due to the fact that the horse breaks over at that point.

At the same time, the leverage of the accumulated bent horn tubules of the unphysiologically rounded part causes distraction to the side. As a result, horn tubules are torn from their bond at the point where those opposing forces collide. This causes vertical cracks and fissures in the hoof wall (orange arrow).

The following picture shows the hoof after the first treatment. Only minutes have passed in between the two pictures. The hoof wall was not filed from below, only rasped from the outside in a specific way, with the Thatched Roof Technique. You can clearly see how the coronary band has relaxed and the entire bone column appears more symmetrical. The bones inside are of course still shaped the same way they were before, but it has been made more comfortable for the horse to stand in his horn shoe. Furthermore, in the future, it will be able to use the hoof differently, which can grow out in the way the bone column inside it determines.

Same hoof, minutes later:

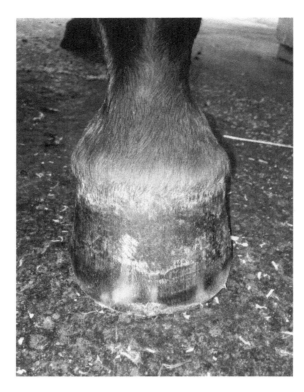

Picture number three shows the hoof one month later. Of course, as a result of the correct treatment, the crack has also grown out:

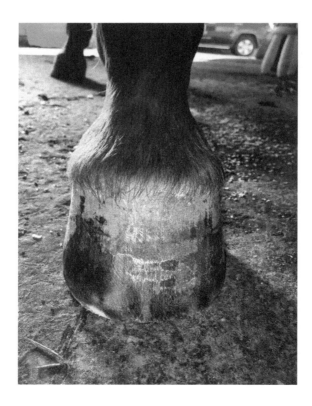

Same hoof, solar view:

Corresponding to what we saw from the dorsal view, the solar view shows how all horn parts are exposed to physical forces. The main load is on the medial side (right in the picture). The frog horn is being pushed to the other side, away from the center of pressure. It leans over the lateral sulcus like a roof. So does the bar on that side, leaning more onto the sole horn. The medial bar is more upright; it is situated under the load. The bearing edge on that side is rounded due to the described flare.

Palmar view:

Due to that main load, the medial hoof wall (left) is much straighter than the lateral. However, the forces work more proximally (upward). Due to those compression forces, the bulb on that side is being pushed upwards also. It seems pointier than the wider lateral bulb.

Example 2:

Left front foot, solar view:

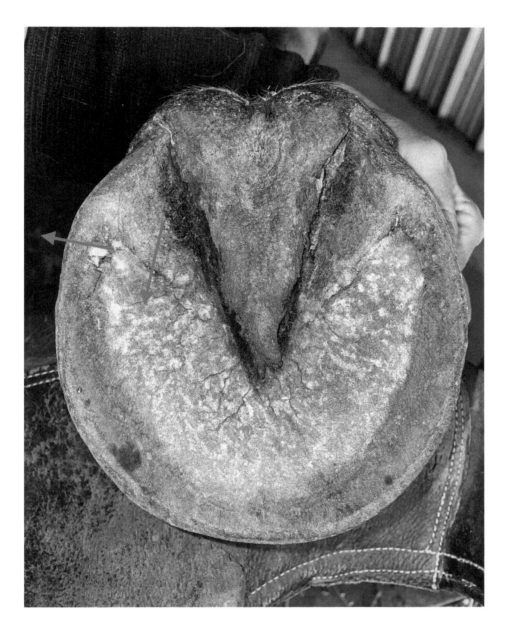

The main load is on the medial side (right in the picture). The medial bar is straighter and the bulb is pushed upwards. The lines show the alignment of the heel horn tubules. The heel wall on the medial side is straighter. The lateral bar leans on the sole, covering the angle of the sole. The construct buttress of heel, bar and heel wall create a firm unit pressing against the bearing edge.

Palmar view:

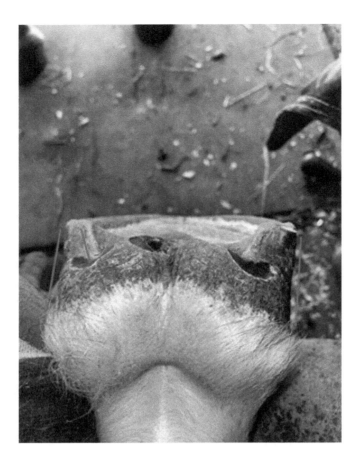

The red lines indicate the different hoof wall length. Due to the medial load and increased abrasion, the hoof wall tubules are shorter on that side. We can see that the bearing edge on the lateral side is slightly longer. It is tempting to cut that off and level it to the other side. But that is not the right way to do it.

Let's go deeper in the matter to explore the correct way.

The following picture shows a right front hoof.

The lateral quarter wall of the hoof (left in the picture) is clearly straighter than the medial quarter wall. The slanted medial side is uncomfortable for the horse to use. Nevertheless, it toes-off on the medial part of the toe wall (blue curve).

We also see horizontal lines that seem to be narrower, more compressed, exactly on those medial hoof wall parts. These rings are often mistaken with growth rings or, as I call them, metabolic rings. Metabolic rings result from any changes affecting the metabolism. Any disorder that burdens the metabolism can influence the horn production. They therefore must have a systemic effect, meaning, they would be visible in all four hooves equally.

Metabolic rings are very often confused with stress rings that result from mechanical forces, affecting each hoof individually. The cause is hoof deformation. They are a clear sign that the hoof is imbalanced.

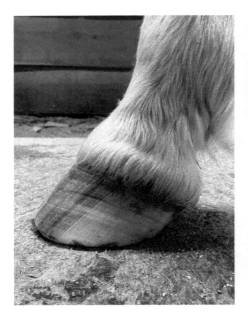

The rings are compressed more in the section of the hoof where the greatest leverage is at work. It is the section that has less load and usage. The horn tubules bend, cannot wear off and simply fold in wrinkles.

The solar view of the hoof clearly shows a main load laterally (right in the picture):

The frog, the left bar, the left bulb are pushed away from the center of the load; They follow the path of least resistance. We can also see that there is no hoof wall length nor bearing edge length to cut off. Even if we wanted, we could not correct that situation by filing anything off the hoof wall from underneath, there is no material. Due to its hoof deformation, the horse is forced to use its whole limb a certain way. We can see how it breaks over the more medial side of its toe instead of the center of the hoof. The picture below was taken four weeks later and it shows the natural abrasion in the toe (blue curve).

The break over point is diagonal from the main load of that hoof. Other hoof wall parts that are not being used become more prominent. The hoof horn accumulates. That accumulated horn becomes an obstacle for the horse to break over when walking, and the hoof deforms even more.

The goal is to give the horse the chance to use this hoof uniformly in order to bring about a more even load.

In the picture below, we can see that the horse favors standing on his left leg:

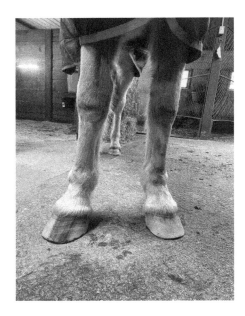

No matter how I tried to position the horse, it would always return into the same favored posture, putting more weight on the left leg and turning the right leg outward.

Similar to the first hoof example, the sloping hoof wall is an unpleasant obstacle for the horse. The horse avoids standing on this levering side. Therefore, it turns the hoof outward to avoid discomfort. Thus, postural anomalies are created in the long run. The whole leg seems twisted, starting in the carpal joint (knee).

This is a photo from directly after treatment:

With the Thatched Roof Technique, the horn tubules in the bent quarter wall have been shaped in a certain way so that together as a bond they can now withstand the ground counterpressure.

This will cause the coronary band to receive different impulses which will change the orientation of the re-growing horn tubules.

Eliminating leverage is only one aspect the hoof specialist needs to address in hoof correction. It is also necessary to determine which parts of the wall should receive more wear in order to balance the hoof. Hoof parts that have less wear will gain more tubule length. The horse in this case toes-off more medially. This leads to accumulated hoof wall length laterally from that abraded toe part. If not corrected, it can deform the hoof even more in the future.

Already after the first treatment the horse is able to place its leg better under the body. The correction process is determined by the horse itself. It will become clear whether it is able to use its limbs differently or whether the bones and joints have already adapted too much to the old posture patterns.

As you can see below, the horse is able to put its leg more under its weight after the first treatment:

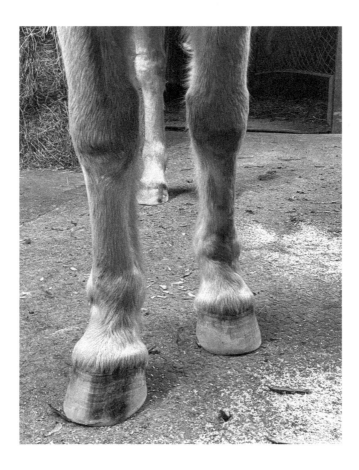

8 weeks later:

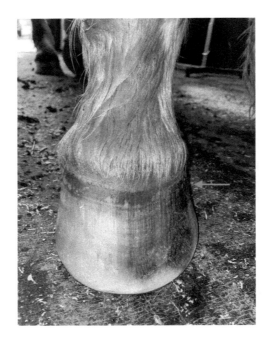

The slanted hoof wall grows down more vertically. The horizontal compression folds disappear, the horn tubules can grow down unhindered. The arrow indicates the change in horn tubule orientation. The lateral toe part has been prepared in order to control the abrasion. The hoof wall has not been cut or rasped from below.

12 weeks later:

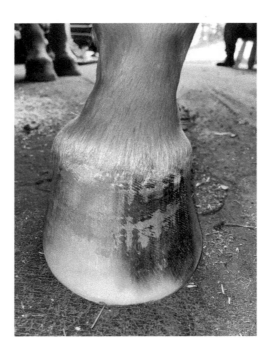

The slant in the medial quarter wall will disappear. Due to the diagonal use, the lateral part of the toe will always have a tendency to become longer and cause compression in the coronet. Therefore, the abrasion on that part needs to be intensified in the future in order to completely balance out the hoof.

The horse will always turn his leg outward due to the already acquired limb deformation, but you can see it puts more weight on it already:

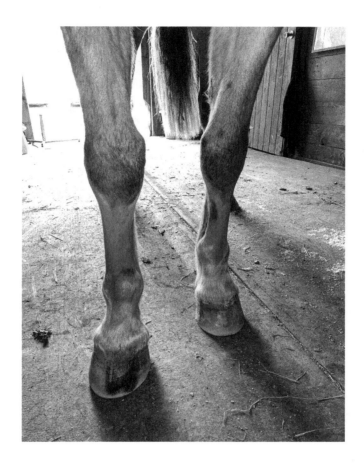

Case 2

Left Hind Foot of a Frisian Mare.

In the next image, it is clearly visible how the coronet-ground distance differs. Medial (left in the picture), the coronet appears dammed up. We see fine horizontal compression folds, in which the dirt sticks. The hoof capsule appears uneven and rough there. Small vertical lines are visible.

The folds are compressed exactly at the point where the coronet appears to be dammed up. They are narrower there than on the other hoof side. There is also a crack that already gaps into the bearing edge.

The hoof a few minutes later, after treatment:

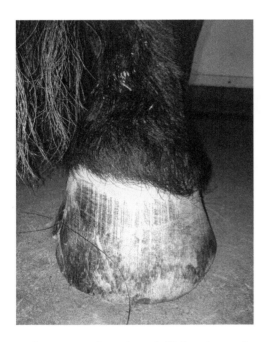
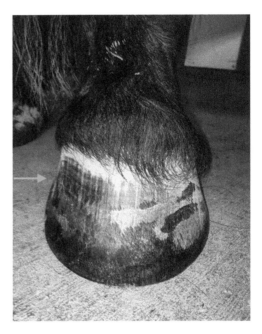

It is now clearly visible that the concise horizontal line (arrow) indicates a change in horn tubule alignment. Below the line, the lever still acts very strongly into the hoof capsule. The crack ends exactly at the line, where the leverage point of the hoof wall is. The hoof wall tries to grow out more vertically but is then pulled outward in the lower part below the indication line.

Because of the leverage, the horse is uncomfortable using this side of the hoof wall. The horse loads the hoof laterally and turns both hind hooves outward to compensate for the greater wall length medially.

The solar view shows the involvement of the bar and the reason why the crack occurred:

The hoof is loaded on the lateral side (left in the picture).

The horn of the frog is being pushed into the opposite direction, away from the pressure, covering the inner sulcus. The right bar seems bigger, more concise. Due to less wear, the bar horn accumulates and lays onto the sole. The hoof shows no excessive bearing edge length. Correction by cutting parts of the hoof wall off is not possible.

If the bar is not properly corrected by cut into the right angle to the ground, it will cause the heel wall to bulge out to the side in an unphysiological way. This again releases opposing mechanics. The flexible heel wall collides with the more rigid quarter wall. If the forces become too strong, the tubules will not be able to withstand the force and will break. In addition, the greater wall length on that hoof wall part increases the leverage forces even more. The heel wall can separate from the quarter wall, as it happened in this case.

The correct angulation and length of the bars is essential. They support the inner laying ungular cartilages. If the bars lose their support function, it can have a negative effect on the cartilages, such as ossification.

The horse will maintain the lateral load for the rest of its life. It is important to achieve the optimal condition, to contain the forces as much as possible and to create a uniform use.

If this succeeds, negative factors can be eliminated.

8 months later:

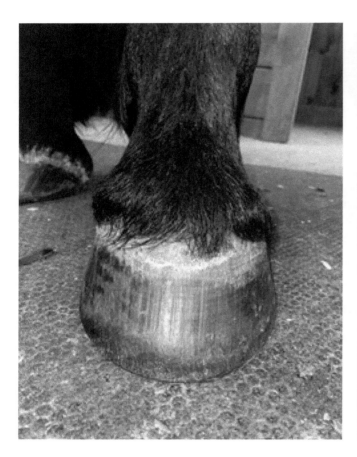 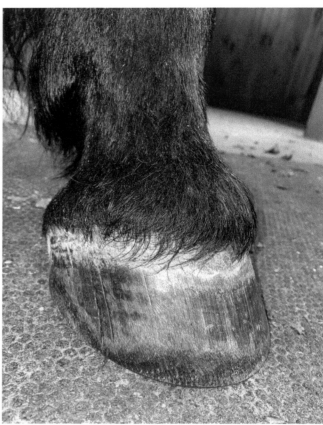

The coronet is almost even now. The gap has closed but a fine vertical line can still be seen. The hoof is not yet rehabilitated.

Below, the front feet are compared after first treatment and 8 months later.

Right Front:

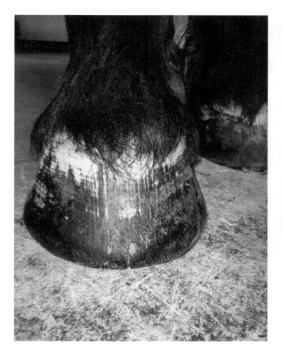 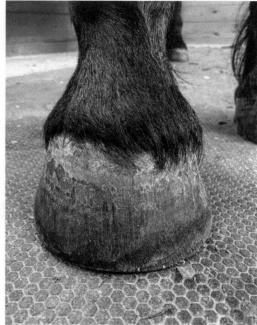

Left front:

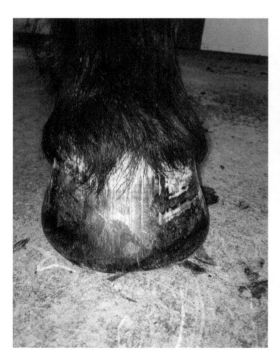 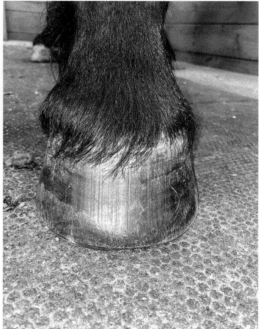

Case 3

Right Front:

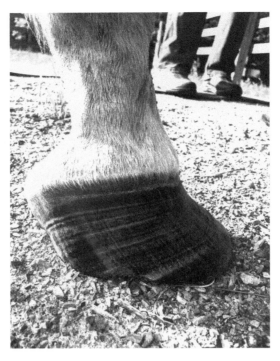

The toe wall is clearly bent to a massive concave. In contrast to the parallel left hoof:

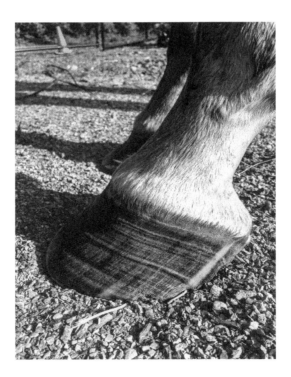

Although the toe wall shows a slight bend here as well, it is not as massive as in the right hoof. How can two hooves develop so differently?

The pictures also show that a previous correction, or the wish to visually adjust the hooves to one another, has failed. The hooves show a different angulation in their hoof-pastern axis. While the left is almost aligned, the right hoof-pastern axis seems to be broken forward (see chapter club foot).

The long pastern bone is slightly steeper than the one of the left hoof.

The green line in the next picture shows how the coffin bone is actually suspended in its hoof. The trained eye can see without an x-ray how the hoof capsule tries to follow its inner structure and grow down aligned to the position of the coffin bone, parallel to it. If you ignore the concave deviation of the toe wall and follow the line of the healthy tubule orientation, you will see how the hoof capsule should actually be shaped.

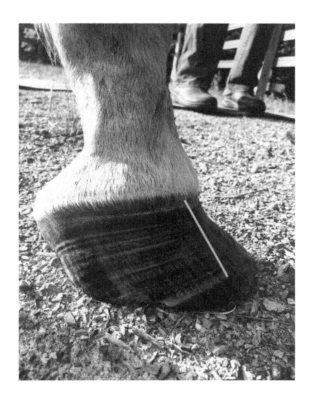

Attempts to optically match both hooves by cutting down the heels of the steeper hoof will inevitably fail. The Deep Digital Flexor Tendon (DDFT) is already shorter than in the other hoof and can no longer stretch. To try to achieve this by manipulating the hoof capsule is nonsensical. The tubules of the toe wall will not be able to withstand the leverage and tensile forces generated by this, as happened in this case.

Not rasping the toe wall correctly made it start to flare over the course of time. The horn tubules bent concavely. This was also the case with the left hoof, just not as severe. It is easier for a flatter angled hoof to adapt to this unphysiologically acquired shape than for a hoof that has a steeper coffin bone. Any bending or deviation of the toe wall from this steep bone alignment acts as a massive lever in the toe wall and is therefore much more severe and problematic in a steep hoof than in an already flat one. The palmar view shows that the tubules of the toe wall were so strongly bent that they did not touch the ground any more. They have an almost horizontal alignment at the end:

The mediolateral balance had also not been corrected in the past:

The limb is heavily loaded medially (right in the picture) and has already deformed accordingly. The medial quarter wall grows down steeply under the load to the point where it is deflected outward from its direction of growth. The entire lateral quarter wall grows out more concavely, fleeing away from the load. Due to the lack of abrasion, this lateral hoof wall has become longer and the tubules fold more because they are not worn down. The lever is strongest in the lower third of the hoof, indicated by a deep strong horizontal groove. As already mentioned, the tubules no longer have any contact with the ground in the toe. The outermost horn tubules lie functionless on the inner tubules; they fan out. Because of this, cracks form in the toe wall. A particularly strong crack can be seen right in the middle of the toe. The tubules are torn from their bond.

The lateral levering quarter wall is very uncomfortable for the horse to stand on. The main load is medial but the levering medial section of the toe wall (red curve) also makes it impossible to put the leg straight under the weight. The poor horse needs to twist that limb and turn it outward in order to be able to stand on it.

7 months later:

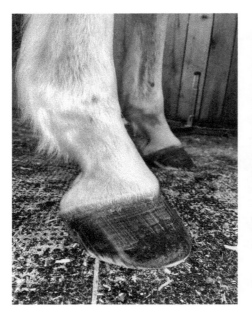 

The hoof is aligned to its steeper pastern. Toe and heel tubules are parallel. The toe wall touches the ground, the hoof has a supporting rim all around.

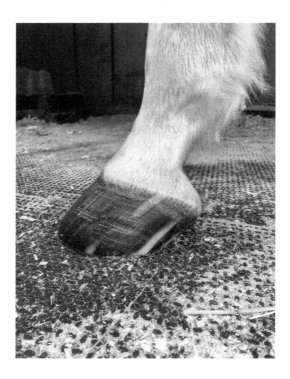

The left foot is aligned too, heel and toe tubules are parallel. This hoof will always be the most loaded and favored hoof. Its hoof-pastern axis will stay hyperextended which is fine! It is the horse's natural acquired situation. The important fact is that the hoof, as the foundation, stays as comfortable and aligned to its coffin bone as possible.

Comparison right front:

Before   7 months later

 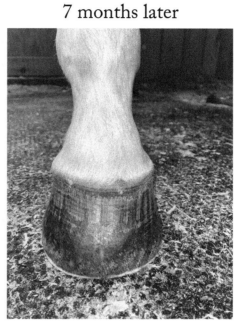

7 months later the horse is able to put its feet straight under the weight, the coronet is even. The hooves are still in rehabilitation but they show much improvement.

Case 4

This beautiful 12-year-old German mare was introduced to me with an old tendon injury in her right front hoof. In the past months she seemed to repeatedly reinjure herself. The Lesion in the Deep Digital Flexor Tendon (DDFT) did not seem to heal.

In order to support the tendon, bar shoes were recommended.

The owner contacted me to find out if improvement of the hoof shape would bring overall improvement for the tendon problem.

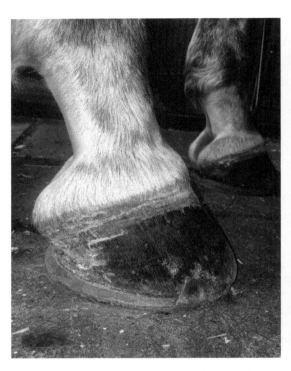 

The left picture shows extremely underrun heels in both hooves. The heel line is far from parallel to the toe line in both feet. The right picture shows the bar shoe that was applied in order to 'protect' the tendon from hyperextending.

I have mentioned the general negative effect of the shoe before in the introduction. A shoe that is closed in the back increases pressure to the hoof capsule even more. The shoe increases the wear of the heel disproportionately.

I think it is unnecessary to explain that a horse with an exterior tendon problem should have the physiological heel height the inner structures stringently require to be protected. Any kind of hyperextension of the DDFT leads to an increasing risk of reinjury and will not promote the recovery process. At the same time, the mediolateral balance is just as important to relieve adjacent joints and ligaments in the process.

Directly after first treatment:

| Right Fore | Left Fore |

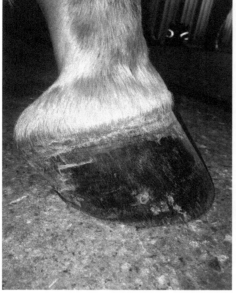 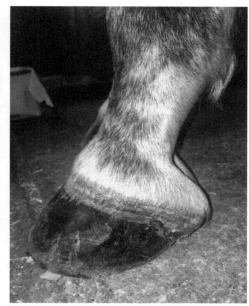

Comparison 4 months later:

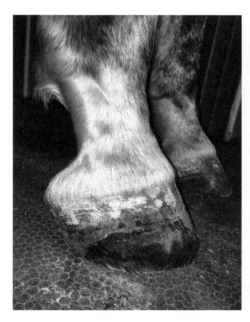 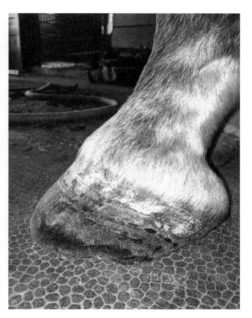

Both hooves seem to align to their pastern, with the heels still underrun. Especially the left hoof (right picture) seems to grow out much steeper in the toe wall. Now being able to distribute weight on the hoof more, the overloaded heels can recover and will get their physiological height as needed. Being able to use the left foot more comfortably, the right hoof, with the tendon problem, gets more relief as well.

By that time, the owner introduced the horse again to the veterinarian for reevaluation. The right front pastern ultrasound showed an unchanged core lesion at the lateral lobe of the DDFT.

The radiographs showed "appropriately balanced feet and significant improvement in right front foot balance since time of initial injury."

The x-rays only showed the hoof pastern alignment, not the mediolateral balance, which to me is as important and improved as well.

Another 3 months later:

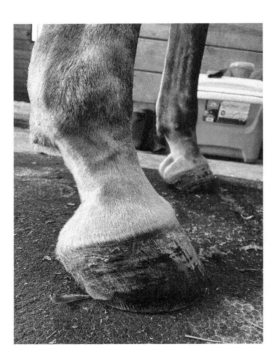 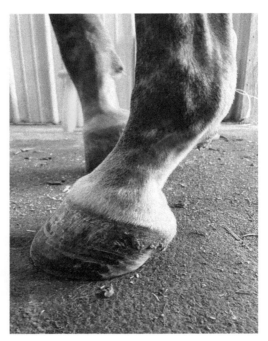

Heel and toe line are parallel

The owner had the Oldenburg-beauty checked again. This time the report stated that the lesion was filled and healed.

This was a very quick and effective recovery in only 7 months compared to the chronic struggles the owner and horse had to experience before for almost 2 years.

The case shows that the bare foot, if given the opportunity with correct treatment, helps itself into the correct shape quicker than with any artificial adjusted device. Only a horse that can feel the surfaces it walks on can take care of its limb as needed.

Case 5

The next case shows a candidate with all four different, terribly distorted feet. You would think the horse had been neglected and not given the luxury of hoof care at all. But it had, in regular intervals.

When the new owner introduced him to me, the poor boy could not walk properly, he didn't know how to use his feet. He had arthritis in his right front carpal joint which leads to a specific hoof shape accordingly. I will discuss 3 of his feet.

Right fore-foot

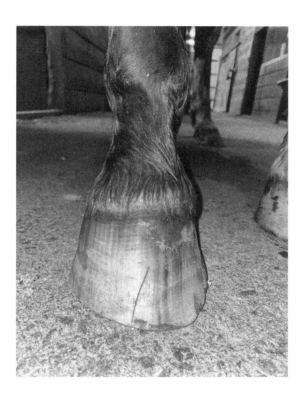

Not knowing the horse's history, it is hard to tell if the terrible hoof shape caused the arthritis in earlier years or if the hoof distortion is a result of the adaption to the arthritis.

The fact is, any change caused by a radical hoof trim would give the little guy and his joint a hard time. So, we do not force him into a new shape; we just make it easier for him to use his leg and let him decide if he wants the changes or not.

Right now, he is forced to only use his lateral toe wall when he lifts his foot. He can't even toe off in the middle. That will influence the swing phase of his leg and his complete movement.

The medial side of the toe has become a huge obstacle that forces the hoof to the lateral side while lifting off. It causes a severe leverage in the coronary band (right where the dirt adheres).

I can hear my dear colleague Angelika in Germany right now: "You know Nadine, you could have cleaned those hooves before you show them in a book."

Yes, I know. I could have cleaned them. Or could it be that I left the dirt there on purpose!? Because there is a reason why it sticks right there, at that spot. And it is not only dirt. What we also see, is a perioplic horn that is not rubbed off, exactly at the area of the hoof wall where the horn tubules are the longest, compressed and folded.

It is the section where the surface of the hoof is very rough. We see compression lines again, the tubules fold and provide perfect structure for the dirt to stick exactly there.

4 weeks later:

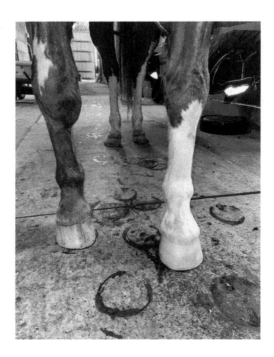

We see the arthritic knee in the previous picture and can imagine how hard it would be for the horse to suddenly not have the supporting length medial on the hoof due to it being cut off.

This time we see no dirt, but we do see the perioplic horn still stuck to the hoof, which proves that most compression is directly in the area with compressed wrinkles. The perioplic horn stays attached and does not rub off.

The coronary band is not as pushed upward; the horse used the middle part more, but not the medial part.

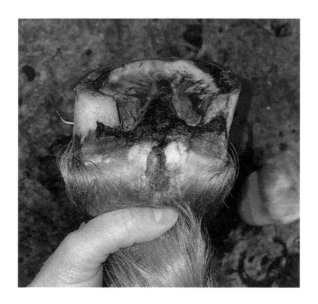

The palmar view shows how the medial hoof wall is longer. The bulbs are relatively the same height, not shifted. The hoof has more tubular horn length on the medial side. The sole horn has the same level all around, like the bulbs.

I know that a lot of trimmers would be itching to cut that excessive hoof wall length off to balance the hoof! No, please don't. He will be in pain. Take a look at the results after treatment:

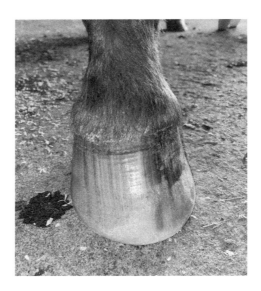

Look how relaxed the coronet looks. I did NOT reduce the length on the medial side. I left the hoof as crooked as it was. However, I did eliminate leverage and compression in the disturbing medial quarter wall. The work starts now. New impulses and dynamics in that hoof wall will lead to different horn tubule growth in a different orientation.

2 months later:

The newly produced hoof wall horn on the medial side can grow down in a new orientation, unhindered in the direction of growth. The horse now uses the whole toe, not only the lateral side.

3 months later:

The coronary band is even. The new horn can grow down unhindered.

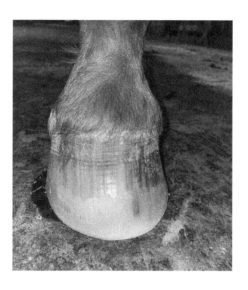

Dorsal view hind feet:

Right Hind   ### Left Hind

   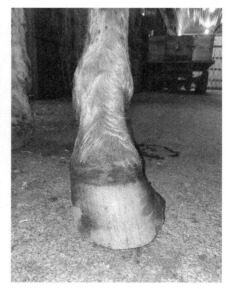

I know Angelika, I know. Despite the dirt we can still see how wonderfully distorted these hooves are. I assume it's not such a wonderful feeling for the poor horse since he is not able to use his lateral quarter walls at all.

1 month after the first treatment:

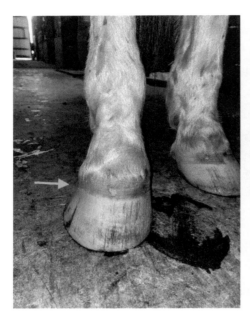
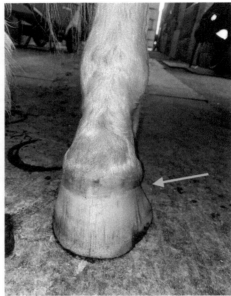

2 months later:

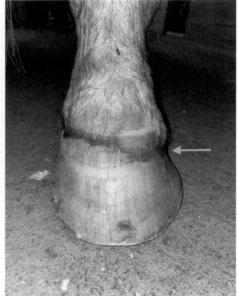

The arrows indicate the different tubule angulation. The difference is incredible, especially in the left hind. Train your eye and ignore the old hoof underneath the indication line. Cover up that hoof wall section with your hand if necessary. Focus on the new growth and imagine how that hoof wants to grow out. Again, the perioplic horn helps you identify the change in angulation. It gets stuck in the indication line. At the moment, it is more compressed and shorter on the lateral side of each hoof. The indication line is much more significant there because of the immense acting leverage the slanted hoof wall is causing.

3 months later:

The hoof grows out straight. The coronary band is more even. The horse can put its leg straighter under his body. Before, the complete leg looked twisted. The lateral leverage caused discomfort; he was not able to use the lateral quarter walls.

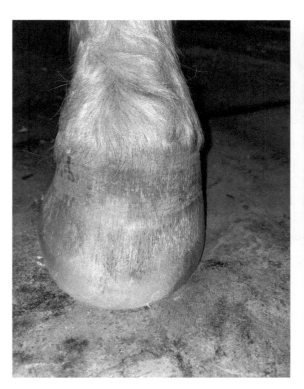 

Plantar view:

Left Hind

Right Hind

We do not have more hoof wall length on the flaring side, although it looks like. The hoof wall length is the same on each side in both hind feet.

The lateral quarter walls with the lateral bulb have only shifted downward. The tubules have bent and lost ground height based on distance from the ground to the coronary band. The actual horn tubule length is the same as on the other side.

How do we 'lift' a collapsed hoof wall? By lowering the other side? Certainly not.

We can accomplish it by changing the usage of that hoof. Once the collapsed flaring hoof walls have grown down vertically steeper, the hoof wall gains height again on that side.

Only 1 month later:

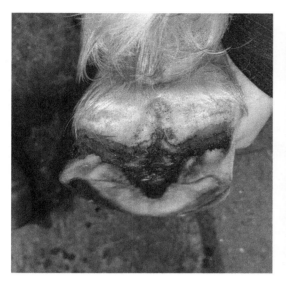
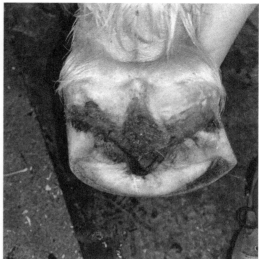

I don't expect the bulbs to be on one level ever due to the medial overload of both hind legs, but after four weeks we already see much improvement.

3 months later:

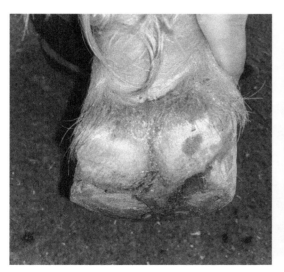
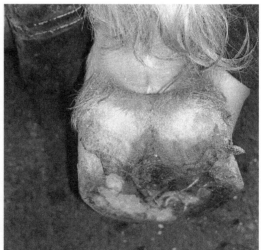

Solar view:

1 month after first treatment:

Both lateral bars lay completely on the sole horn, are collapsed and have no supporting function for the ungular cartilage anymore. We can imagine how they are co-responsible for pushing the lateral heel and quarter wall outward. However, if not cut back the right way, (meaning in a way that they have a supportive function and can withstand the ground reacting forces), their horn tubules accumulate and cover up the heel angle. In the long run, that will add to the tensile forces already happening in the flaring quarter wall. Cutting that bar off completely would be a big mistake. That bar would only collapse more in the future while growing out.

Let's have a closer look at the right hind:

This time, the dirt is very helpful. The blue arrow shows how on exactly that side and it is ONLY there that the dirt and little stones are able to stick, working their way up due to the main load. Whereas on the other side, the forces push the horns outward and not upward. Those are two different forces. While shear forces are working on the left side in the picture, tensile forces work on the right side.

The yellow arrows indicate the direction into which all involved horn parts are being pushed, into the path of least resistance. The lamellar layer on the right side is also covered by sole horn and stretched, whereas it won't be stretched at all on the left side. It cannot be. There is no pulling to the side (tensile forces), only proximal pushing. Shear forces work the dirt deep into a created cavity. I will discuss this topic further in the sections 'White Line Disease' and 'Hoof Wall Cavity'.

The picture of the cleaned hoof, cut but not filed yet, confirms what I explained before. We see the stretched lamellar layer and widened golden line on the right side but a completely intact and thin lamellar layer and golden line on the left side. The golden line is not golden anymore, it is red now. The lamellar layer, on the other hand, is intact, whereas on the right side, the golden line and lamellar layer are enlarged, stretched. The individual horn parts are no longer clearly distinguishable from each other. That complete side, up to the toe is yellow, reddish, discolored.

Due to the tensile forces the dermis reacts to the ongoing irritation and secretes plasma or hemoglobin into the horn at the origin of production. It is a sign of stress, not a bruise, as it is commonly called. A bruise would be trapped behind the horn, not within the horn. Did you ever hit your thumb? The bruise appears behind the nail, not in the nail. Otherwise, most shod horses would have red and purple hooves every time the farrier hits the hoof capsule with the hammer when shoeing your horse.

I call it horn discoloration. It is an indicator that something has stressed the corium.

On the left side of the hoof, all the forces work upward. Those shear forces separate the hoof wall tubules from the origin of the lamellar layer, the weakest part where tubule horn turns into lamellar horn. Neither the dirt nor bacteria are responsible for causing that, only hoof mechanics.

4 weeks later:

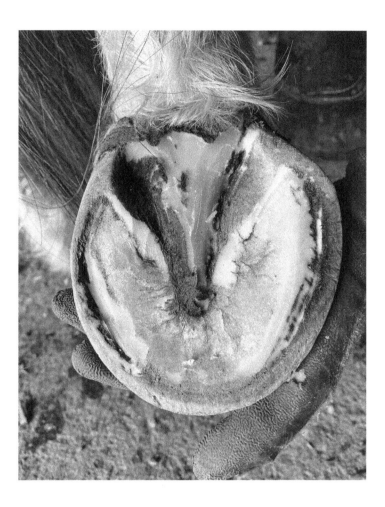

The cavity on the left will close up soon because I gave the horse the possibility to use the other side of the hoof as well, which it gladly accepted. The bar on the lateral side is more stable and doesn't lean as much on the sole anymore. There is no discoloration in the toe. That's a good first step.

This case can be followed on **www.hoofphysics.com**

Case 6

In the following case, the two examples cover a lot of hoof problems or better said, symptoms, in the two hooves presented.

The main cause for all those problems is simply hoof imbalance, distortion. We will see white line and cavity syndrome, cracks, abscesses and keratomas. The mare was introduced to me lame on her right front. The owner wasn't sure where exactly the lameness was coming from.

Right Fore

Left Fore

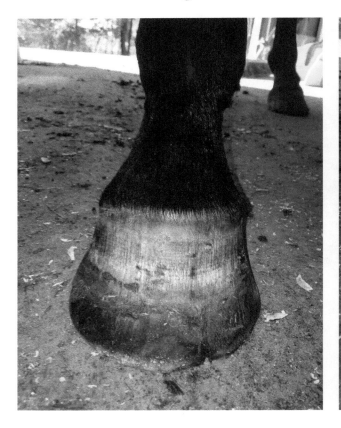

We see two front hooves with similar symptoms. They both try to grow out smaller, steeper and then the hoof walls deviate from the coffin bone all around after the first third of growth. Without seeing the solar view, it should be obvious that the lamellar layer must be stretched all the way around. It's a perfect entry for bacteria, but that's not what caused the lameness.

Left Front:

The arrows show not only how deep the dirt and bacteria dug their way in between the hoof wall and lamellar layer (cavity) but also affected the stretched areas of lamellar horn (white line disease). I will explain the difference in its respective section.

This hoof is loaded most on the medial side (right in the picture) but had extreme pressure in the complete heel part due to the girl's natural broken back hoof-pastern line. The flare in the toe made the problem worse and pushed the weight even more towards the heels.

After cleaning the affected areas and removing dirt and bacteria with copper sulfate, it was also important to fill the cavities to avoid new stones and dirt to get in. Bee's wax is an excellent choice for that. The cavities were only the symptoms of the real cause: The distorted shape of the hoof.

The other foot was the sore foot:

The pain came from the lateral heel (arrow). There was no exudate, no acute abscess. The pressure to the corium caused by dirt deeply stuck between the hoof wall and lamellar layer caused the lameness. This hoof is loaded on the lateral side. That's why that heel was affected more; the dirt was pressed deeply into the hoof.

Both hooves were contracted at the heels.

2 months later:

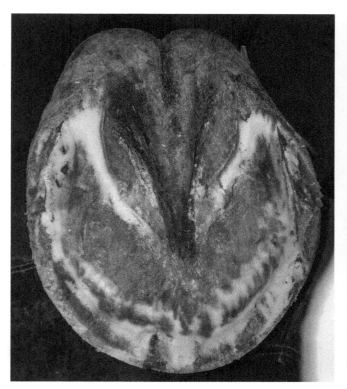 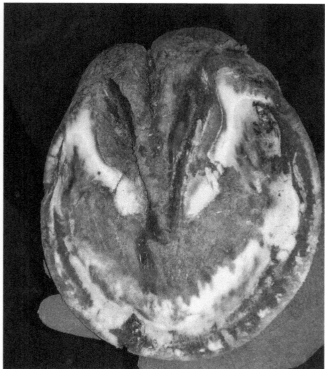

With a new shape growing down, the gaps were able to close up.

The reddish color in the gaps is old horn discolored with hemoglobin. The corium was so irritated that it released hemoglobin into the freshly produced horn tubules. It shows how much pressure those heels had to endure.

The hoof shape improves but the girl still has a lot of pressure on her heels.

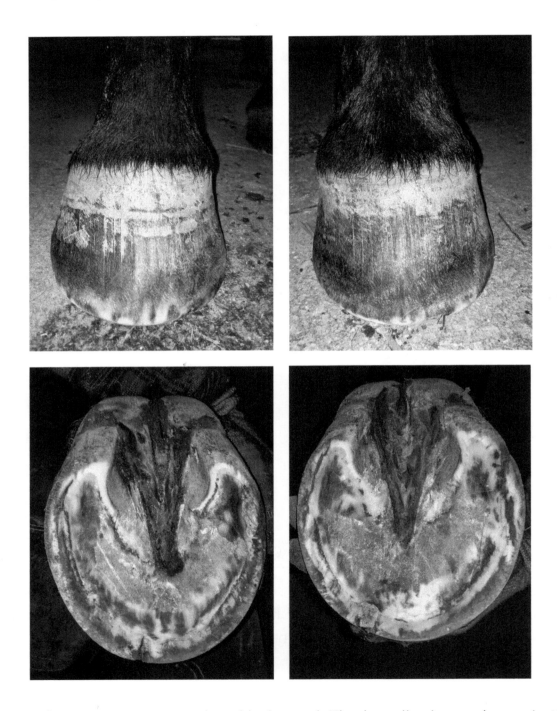

The hooves become more round and balanced. The lamellar layer closes. In the right foot, the rest of the disconnected section of hoof wall and lamellar layer in the lateral heel is growing out.

In the left foot, there is still a little cavity in the medial wall. This time I put chewing gum in it. It is the perfect cheap solution to fill a gap. Yes, chewing gum. Don't worry. Later you will learn how to use sauerkraut to pull an abscess… Bear with me.

Both feet show a gap in their lamellar layer of the toe, starting in the golden line, gapping into the bearing edge. These gaps were caused by keratomas (see section Keratoma).

One year later:

Right Front   Left Front

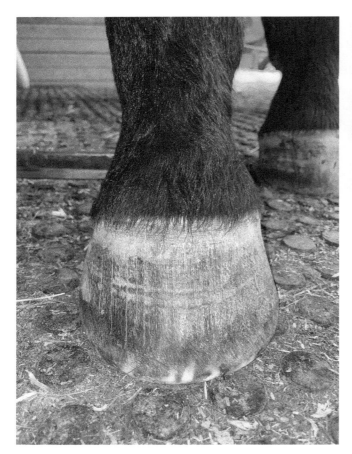 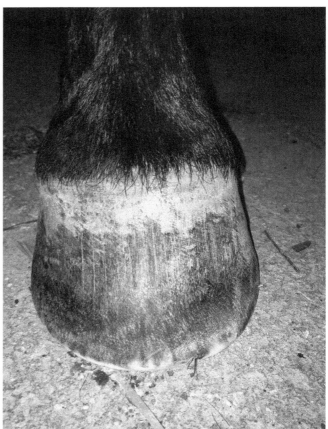

Case 7

The poor boy shown next was born with very small feet in relation to his body. He is a quarter horse and like a lot of quarter horses was bred to look pretty. He has small feet under a very muscular body. Hmmmm... that doesn't work.

The hooves of this boy remind me more of soda cans than hooves. Thank you, mankind.

The pictures start with the second treatment. The first night I was introduced to him, he could not walk due to an abscess. It was dark, and we opened up the abscess in the paddock. I did not take any pictures.

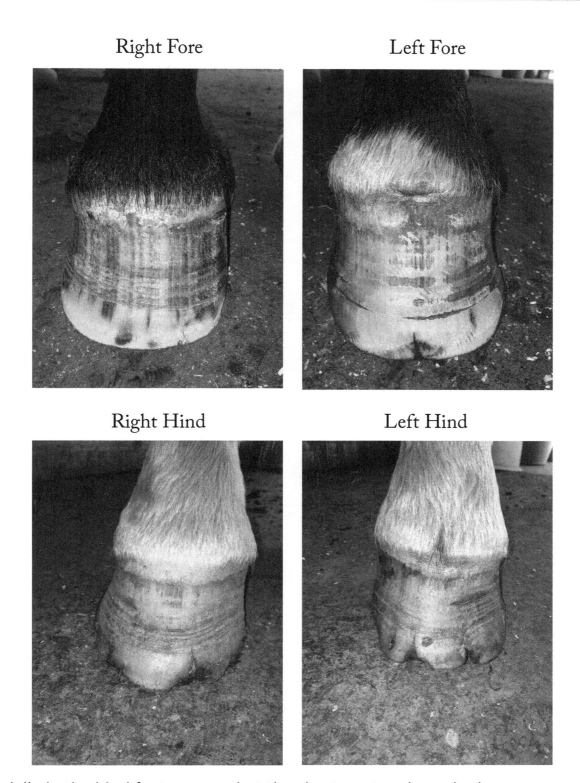

Right Fore   Left Fore

Right Hind   Left Hind

Especially in the hind feet we see that the short pastern bone looks disproportionately bigger than the hoof, the way the hoof wants to grow out. And it is bigger than normal because he has a little tiny coffin bone in his hoof. The hoof capsule only tries to follow what is given by nature – or in this case what mankind created. If we try to make the hoof look bigger, we will fail in that attempt and the horse will suffer.

All hoof walls on all feet were extremely bent with quarter and toe walls flaring away from their coffin bone. In the front, the stressed and stretched lamellae offered entry for bacteria. The horse suffered from recurring abscesses. In the hind feet, the stressed lamellae reacted with the formation of keratomas, which as a result caused the cracks in the hoof wall.

Not only was the white line affected, he also had cavities between the hoof wall and lamellar layer.

4 months later:

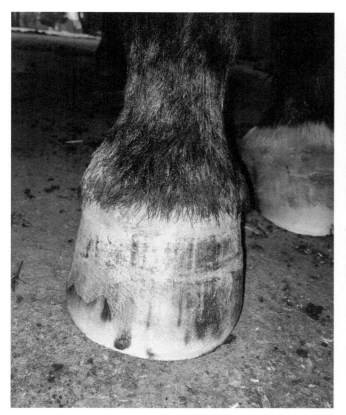 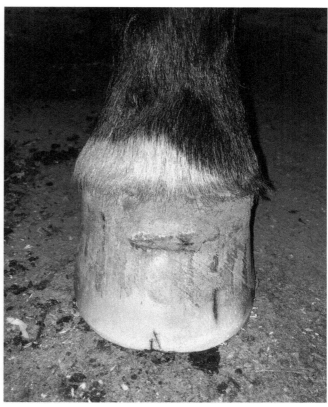

The overall hoof shape is more balanced. Cracks and gaps can grow out.

Hind feet:

The permanent tensile forces in the toe of both hind feet have left their mark.

 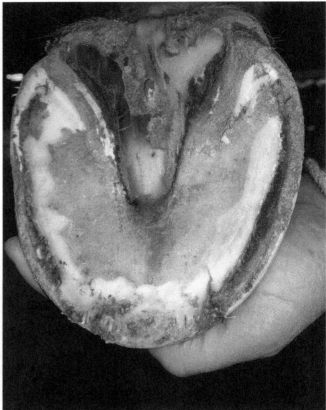

The margin of the coffin bone no longer has a clear structure. Even without radiographs, this is clearly recognizable by the uneven horn structures in the distinction between sole horn, white line and lamellar layer. In both feet, it looks as if all (normally clearly separated) horn parts overlap into each other. The line of the sole edge is no longer even, everything looks blurred and the lamellar layer is widely stretched. Due to small defects in the bone, the adjacent dermis has to adapt to the bone's shape. A space between the dermal lamellae and the hoof wall is created. In order to bridge the space, the corium has to fill it with proliferated horn mass, a kind of scar horn. (See section Keratoma)

I also noticed that the sweet boy never put weight on the heel of his left hind foot, only in the toe. It seemed to be uncomfortable, his fetlock was often stocked up. He was never lame but stiff according to his high age. He grew more heel length in that hoof to support his inner structures. Due to the fact that he loved standing on his toe wall, it was mandatory to not let the hoof wall flare in the toe.

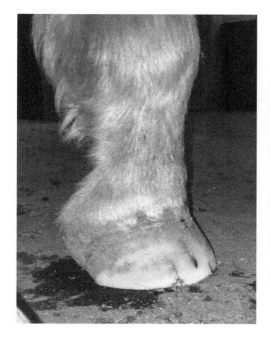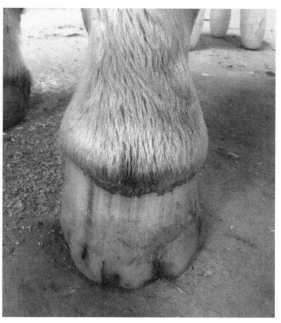

He decided his comfortable heel height. Shortening the heel would make it float in the air. It would not touch the ground and would make him uncomfortable.

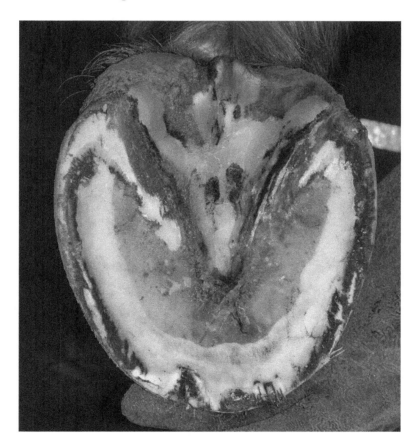

The gaps were still very concise.

1 year later:

 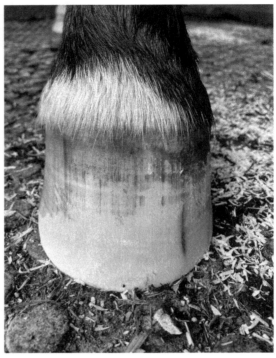

The front feet had recovered a long time ago, but I was still on a mission to close the keratoma areas in the back:

 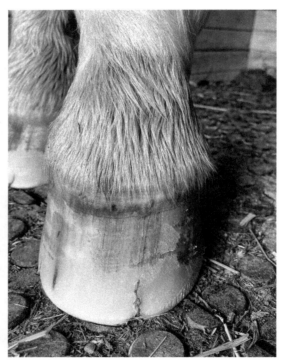

I saw the cracks decreasing, so I had hope I could restore both hind hooves completely. It was a long journey but after 1.5 years all hooves were fully recovered:

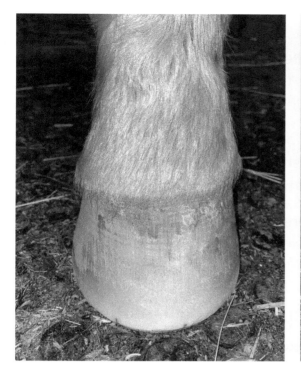
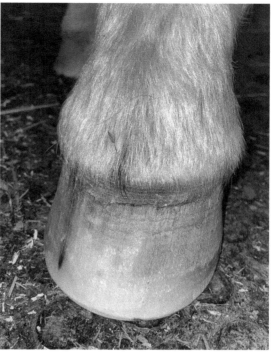

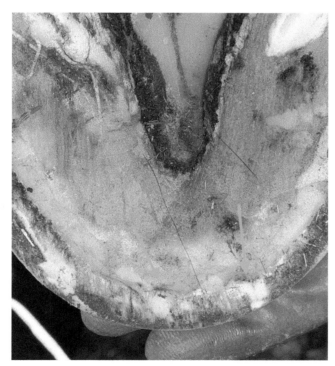

The keratomas will never go away because the bone defect will stay, but as we can see in the picture, it is manageable!

Case 8

The next case is provided by my dear colleague Angelika, owner of the Hoof Orthopedic Center in Cologne, Germany. The case shows her own horse and it is the reason why she became a hoof orthopedist 20 years ago.

Her horse struggled from frog canker on all 4 hooves over 5 years. Canker arises from long-lasting horn macerations, thrush, in connection with accompanying unfavorable hoof conditions, which favor the ingress of anaerobic bacteria.

Because of this, the disease begins preferentially in the deeply furrowed central sulcus of the frog and can spread to the surrounding regions. The infectious process causes a chronic hypertrophy (enlargement or increase) of the horn-producing tissues, the papillae or/and lamellae, but the cells do not keratinize. The result is a thin, moisty horny layer that only dries out on the outside.

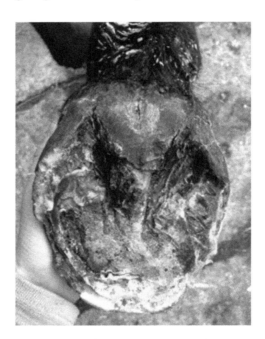

Canker is a very persistent disease of the dermis which cannot be defeated without restoring a healthy hoof shape. Angelika tried a variety of hoof trimming techniques, ointments, medications and consultations of 5 different veterinarians.

Documented is the left fore foot:

 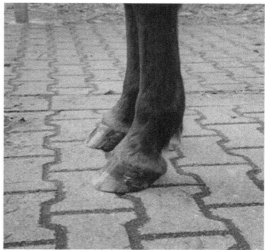

The too flat hoof position results in a broken back hoof-pastern axis. The dorsal hoof wall flares out and does not take up any load.

The collapsed heels clinch the diseased hoof frog and literally squeeze it together. The frog is severely constricted as a result. The frog horn folds. The tiny folds provide entry points for bacteria. This favors the development of decay processes. In addition, the compression of the frog creates a horn ridge which, when pressed into the deep frog furrow, further irritates the dermis there. The dermis, thus put under constant stress, has no chance to heal and continues to produce abnormal horn despite meticulous cleanliness and symptom treatment with various care products.

When introduced to Hoof Orthopedic treatment in 2002, Angelika finally found the answers why the hooves couldn't recover. For the first time in her horse's medical history, the non-physiological hoof situation was addressed as the cause of the hoof disease!

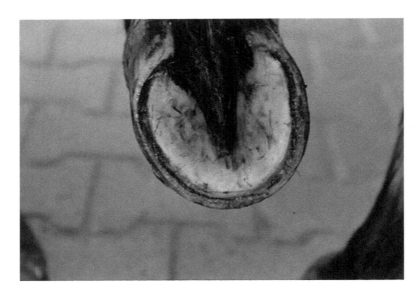

The hooves were treated in 14 days intervals. Only 1.5 months later, the compressed heels opened up, the hoof shape changed and the irritated dermis can heal.

5 months later:

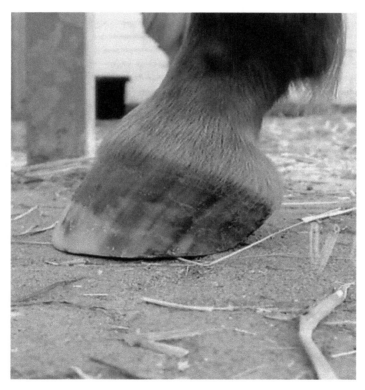

A completely new hoof. The other three hooves developed accordingly.

Chapter 3:
Hoof Diseases · Abscess

Case 1

Right Front Hoof

 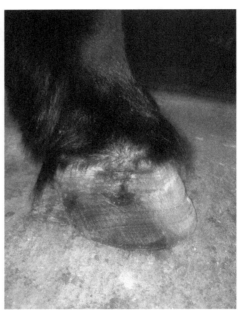

This Friesian Mix suffered from recurring abscesses. We see 3 abscesses in the pictures that broke through the coronet. The horse was not lame anymore when it got referred to me, but the owner was wondering why the horse got one abscess after the other, only on the same foot. I told her that the hoof shape is crucial in this case as in most cases.

We see that the coronary band is bulged out on the lateral side (left in picture) of the hoof.

The hair stands out, breaks, unlike the other side, where it lays over the hoof capsule and grows down.

Of course, the coronary band on the left side is bulging due to the opening left by the abscess, but why exactly at this spot? Was the coronary band may be already bulging out before the abscess came through?

Abscesses are formed when hoof pathogens, specifically bacteria found in feces, called fusobacteria, enter the horn and become trapped. Since these fusobacteria are anaerobic, they love horn areas that provide them with an oxygen-poor climate such as clefts, horn niches and especially the lamellar layer of the suspensory apparatus of the hoof. Bacteria can also enter where a lot of horn accumulates and there may be load imbalances, e.g., on the sole, preferably under the bars.

The affected horns are eaten away, macerated and liquefied bacterially. A foul-smelling exudate is produced, pressing on the corium and usually causing a significant amount of pain.

The corium itself is affected only indirectly, as it is primarily the horns that are decomposed. If the situation remains unchanged for a long time because of incorrect treatment, the corium can also become inflamed down to the bone underneath it. In those cases, pus bacteria can develop.

In this case, the bacteria have repeatedly affected the lamellar layer and there is a reason why.

Trapped behind the massive hoof wall, they can only find a way out at the softest spot, at the coronary band. Sometimes they eat their way further to the side into the sole horn. Then the core abscess can be opened up more swiftly.

Since they are anaerobic, only one remedy helps: air.

The abscess must be opened or you can simply wait until it has found its way out on its own.

The opening of an abscess is the responsibility of the veterinarian. He/she should be consulted and together with the hoof practitioner determine the course of treatment. Unfortunately, in many instances, abscesses aren't treated the right way. The administration of a non-steroidal anti-inflammatory agent is one aspect that does not help to speed up the process. Anti-inflammatory agents make the abscess encapsulate even further and the outbreak is suppressed.

It is always an advantage if the abscess can break through by itself. The pain vanishes immediately after. Soaking the horn, permanently, not just three times 15 minutes a day, will accelerate the ripening of the abscess. A moist, warm environment must be created. The softer the horn, the easier it is for the abscess to penetrate it. Simple warm soapy water or sauerkraut are quite sufficient for this. Yes, sauerkraut. It has an antibacterial and drawing effect. An easy 97 cent solution to the problem.

A lot of horse owners already have experience with abscesses and know how to soak. The abscess usually breaks through after a couple of days. If it is necessary to cut the abscess open, it is important to remove only the affected part of the horn, not complete sections of the hoof wall of the hoof capsule. This would unnecessarily destabilize the hoof.

Now, let us get back to our case. Both quarter walls flare outward. Although the main load of this hoof is medial (right in the picture), the medial quarter wall seems bent, not straight as it should be under the load. The lateral wall seems to grow down straighter in the upper 3rd and starts flaring too after that.

The first abscess happened approximately 6 months ago and caused a huge horizontal gap in the hoof wall (picture dorsal view). The bent medial quarter wall causes distractive forces to the side that work against the toe wall. The tubules can't withstand these opposing forces and are torn out of their bond vertically at the weakest point, exactly where the abscess cut through the hoof wall. The bacteria broke through the coronary band 6 months ago, right where the tubules are being produced.

Because the connective tissue has been eaten by bacteria, a cavity is left behind between the hoof wall and the dermal lamellae, which must grow out completely. If existing negative distractive forces such as a flaring hoof wall are not being controlled, the condition will not be healed. New bacteria can easily enter into the open gap and infest newly produced horn. The next abscess is on its way.

The coronet on the lateral side was already bulging out before the first abscess occurred. Due to lack of abrasion, the hoof has a longer lateral quarter wall.

If not brought into balance permanently, the longer tubules will continue to cause leverage and make the coronet bulge. If the leverage becomes too much, those bent hoof walls will lead to a stretching of the epidermal lamellae, which again offers the perfect access for bacteria.

The picture from the side shows the folds caused by the lever. The horn tubules fold due to compression. The stress lines fold in an arch that has its highest point exactly where the last two abscesses have broken through. Is this a coincidence? No, it's physics. It's the spot with the most leverage.

From a solar view it becomes clear how twisted the hoof has become due to these negative acting forces (Arrows).

The hoof only 5 months later, much more balanced:

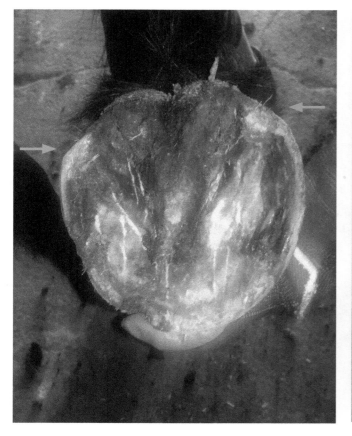

The arrow indicates the last abscess that broke through 5 months ago. It is now clearly visible how steep the sidewalls want to grow down. The newly produced tubules above the abscess grew down in a firm bond. The coronary band is even, balanced.

The discrepancy of angulation between the new and old tubule horn is immense. The horse will grow a completely newly shaped hoof. None of my clients' horses that suffered from recurring hoof wall abscesses before had an abscess again after I balanced out their hoof shape.

It is now clear why the abscess affected only one hoof and especially this one. The horse has two differently shaped front hooves, the left one is flatter and the right one is steep and higher. Tensile forces acting on those steep side walls have a greater tearing effect on the lamellar layer; an easy access for bacteria.

6 months later:

This case can be followed on **www.hoofphysics.com**

Case 2

This is the horse of my dear colleague Nina Seckel in Germany. Nina has been working as a hoof orthopedist since 2016. Her horse Pauli developed Equine Metabolic Syndrome and later on Cushing's in the past 6 years.

Three months before these pictures were taken, unfortunately, she had an episode of laminitis. Nina addressed it the right way and treated the hoof correctly. Pauli improved well from the episode and was not lame anymore until the next two months.

Since the lamellae are compromised after a laminitis episode, it often occurs that bacteria finds its way into the affected area. Pauli developed an abscess on her left front.

Nina started soaking and digging where she assumed the bacteria entered the lamellae. To be assured, she let the vet take an x-ray.

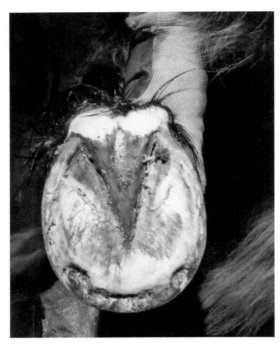

The x-ray showed where the bacteria entered (arrow) and where it was 'eating' its way to the heel, about to exit in the lateral bulb.

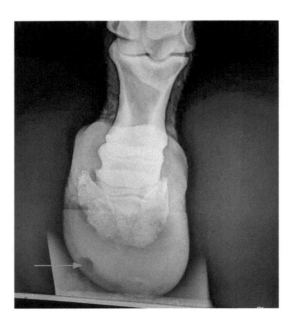

I told her to keep on soaking the hoof. The bacteria most likely undermined the sole horn under the lateral bar.

Four days later parts of the bacteria came out at the bulb and lateral coronary band. The extent of this huge abscess was now visible.

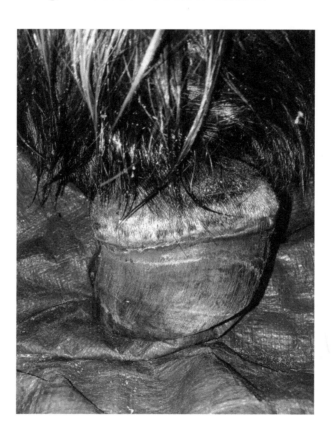

I told her to use all her courage and remove excess horn from the sole, otherwise she won't get rid of the bacteria and it will cause further damage. The only measure that helps to make the horse feel better is to dry out the affected areas. New horn can only be produced if the corium is not being irritated or wet.

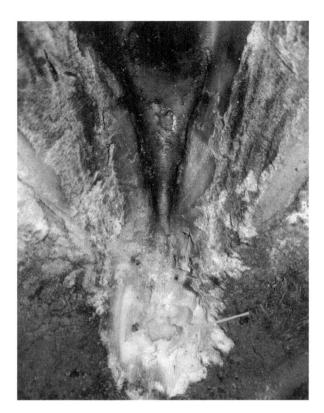

Nina started digging...the frog horn was undermined. The unconnected horn came off easily. The bacteria made its way into the sole horn.

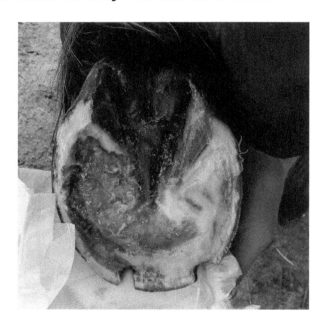

Between the last two pictures only minutes have passed. You can clearly see how fast the frog has dried and the new horn has hardened once exposed to air. In the case of an abscess as severe as this one the corium is extremely irritated and reacts with bleeding to even the slightest touch.

Pauli immediately stood better on her hoof. The pressure was gone.

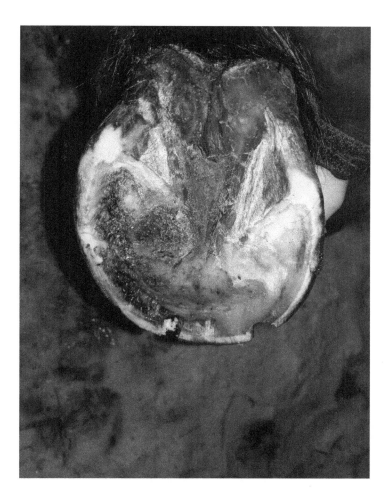

Nina kept the hoof in a diaper for another day but then left the hoof completely open to let it dry. Her horse lives in very clean outdoor boarding conditions.

Pauli could choose how much she wanted to use her foot. Only two days later, Pauli walked much better.

Nina had to then take care of the lever that made the hoof wall flare more on the lateral side (left in the picture). Like in the case before, there is a reason why the bacteria chose to enter in that exact spot. It has the greatest leverage which causes the most tear in the lamellae. Pauli loads her limb on the medial side. The less loaded lateral side flares away from the center of pressure. The lamellae on that side are being stretched more and horn parts accumulate, leaving attack surface for bacteria in those horns.

But Pauli is in the best hands with Nina.

Two days later, the new horn layers protect the sole:

4 weeks later:

We will discuss Pauli's hoof later again in the section Laminitis.

Case 3

Words cannot express the abnormality of the following constructions:

Right Front Hoof   Left Front Hoof

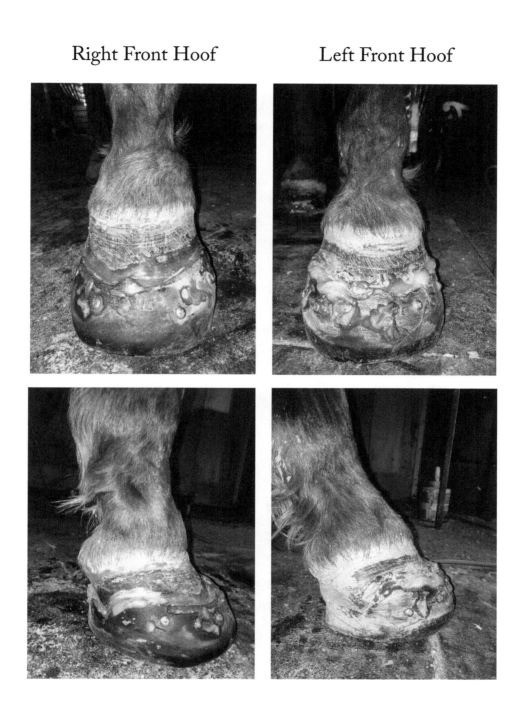

When the horse was introduced to me it was limping in the left front, not knowing how to use her feet at all with these artificially enlarged 'walking aids'.

I was told she got those shoes because she had an abscess in the left front. In order to 'protect' the hoof from mud and bacteria, these special shoes were applied.

It took me a while to take them off, because I had to be careful to not rip the whole hoof wall apart. They were glued AND screwed into the horn. The more the better, I guess...I had an idea why the horse was still limping. I was sure the abscess was still trapped in that monster shoe or at least horn parts that irritated the corium had not been removed. The palmar view confirmed my assumption. The bacteria came out in the bulbs/frog. That meant disturbing, repelled horns were still covering the affected areas.

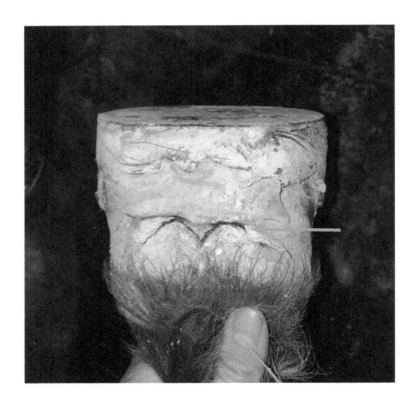

Taking the cover off, I found black stinking macerated horn, and horse manure trapped inside. The perfect unhygienic environment for an abscess to grow.

Parts of the hoof wall did not survive the torture of glue and screws, but that was not the main problem of this poor girl.

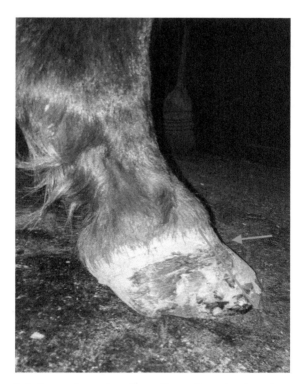

The arrow shows from which point the hoof wall tubules leave their healthy orientation parallel to the coffin bone. That's how they try to grow down (red line) but then are deviated from their physiological alignment.

Same with the right foot:

Lateral View   Medial View

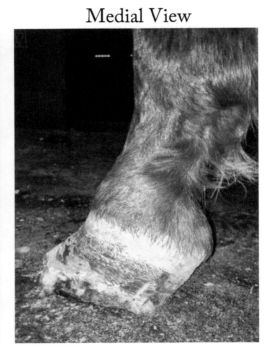

This is a much steeper hoof than the left one, a club foot. The arrow indicates how kinked the tubules are. They try to grow down aligned to the coffin bone that is suspended in the hoof capsule with a natural flexion in the coffin joint (see section Club Foot). The flare deflects from their original orientation.

The sole showed macerated horn (black spots). I expected the whole sole to be undermined. Luckily, the bacteria found their way out through the bulbs and not through the lamellae up to the coronet.

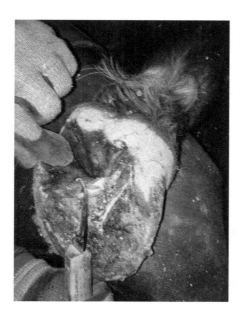

The frog horn was completely loose, newly produced horn peeking out and pushing forward the old material, in between the trapped bacteria.

As expected, a little tiny indicator shows where the abscess found its way into the hoof.

The arrow shows a so-called crena.

When the margin of the coffin bone has a little notch (arrow), the dermal lamellae will follow that shape of the coffin bone while the hoof wall grows down in its original orientation.

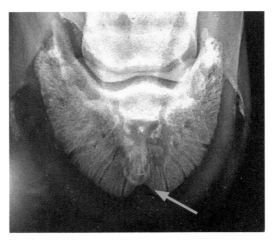

A gap is created between the lamellae and the horn tubules. This little notch in the bone is always in the middle of the toe in the case of a crena. It occurs because of tensile forces or pressure at the breakover point of the hoof due to long-existing deformations and flare in the toe wall.

The more leverage the toe wall experiences, the more the lamellae get stretched. Again, to avoid future abscesses, we need to address the cause, which is the hoof's deformation.

Three days later:

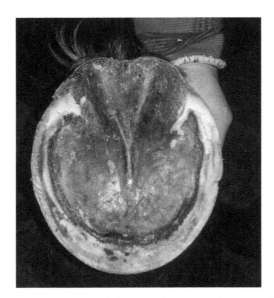

After removing the complete sole and frog, the newly produced horn underneath dried up nicely. We did not cover it up at all. The horse was turned out as usual. I left a higher bearing edge to protect the sole. The horse was lame-free after the first day already. The arrow shows where the abscess started to work. It left a hole in the lamellar layer and the golden line, which will close up in the next months with the right treatment.

The arrows indicate signs of distortion.

4 weeks later:

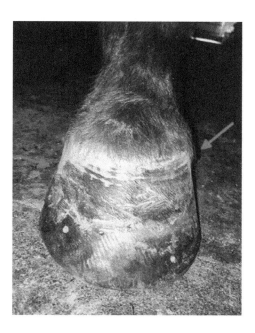

6 weeks later:

Right Front   Left Front

The mediolateral balance is almost achieved. But the hoof is not rehabilitated yet.

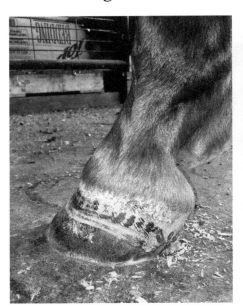 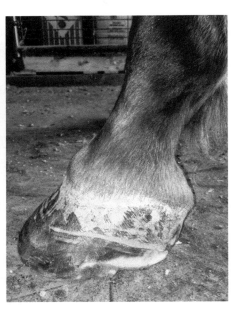

The flare in the toe has only grown out half way. It still causes a lot of leverage and distracts the newly produced horn tubules in their orientation.

It is now visible how much more the left, flat foot was suffering. While the right one recovers quickly, the left seems to struggle with the immense lever. It is the more loaded hoof. More load means more distortion and more problems. Within a short amount of time, the horse would have gotten the next abscess.

The crena could not close yet due to the flare.

The crena closed up, but it is important to keep an eye on the area. The sole horn must be cut back. It must be prevented from 'leaning' over the golden line and the epidermal lamellae which would cover this area, and again would provide great conditions for unwanted bacteria. The yellowish color (blood plasma) shows that the area is still stressed. It needs to be protected. If I were to remove the bearing rim in this area and instead leave the sole horn thicker, it would not solve the problem. The bacteria would still find their way into the hoof.

Right Hoof	Left Hoof

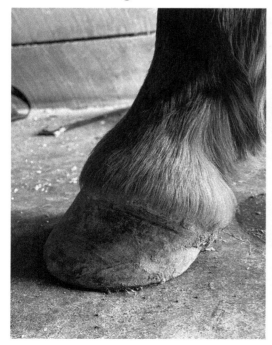
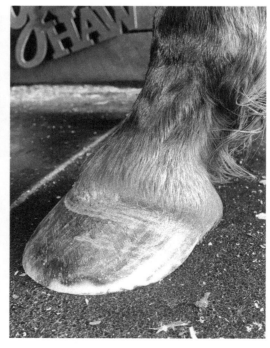

Case 4

Due to an old injury, this 26-year-old Appaloosa gelding had a scar across the medial bulb of his left front foot, reaching into the coronary groove, causing a disruption in horn tubule production in the damaged area of the corium. Instead of proper tubule horn, the corium produces horn which differs in function and consistency from normal tubule horn ('scar horn'). It is less functional and therefore represents a weak point in the statics of the hoof. If the hoof is treated properly, this weak point does not cause any further problems.

In this case, the scar horn in the hoof wall was mistakenly diagnosed as a keratoma, causing an irritation of the scarred skin on the bulb. The horse was lame and shod.

Subsequently, the scar material in the bulb was cut out, leaving the horse with the result seen in the picture.

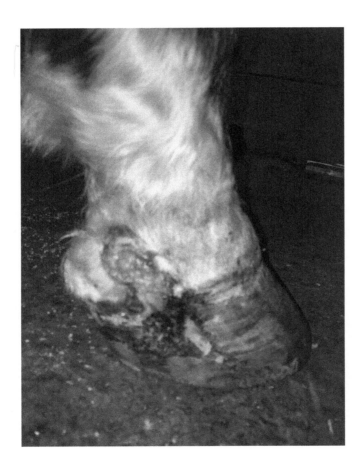

When I saw the hoof, the first thing I looked at were the statics:

The hoof's main load is on the left side in the picture. The side with the scar. It is clearly visible how compression forces work into the coronet, leaving a little roof behind (arrow). The coronet bulges out and the hoof tries to grow down in a completely different angle but it cannot. The tubules are being clinched in their direction of growth. I also noticed a little gap at the medial bulb, right between skin and horn tubules, confirming my suspicion that the horse had nothing more than an abscess. I assumed the whole medial heel was undermined with bacteria which of course caused the lameness in the first place. Applying quantities of different non-steroidal anti-inflammatories kept the abscess cozy and comfortably trapped within the hoof capsule.

The next picture shows the deviation of bulb level. The medial bulb (left in the picture) is pushed upward, the lateral hoof wall has sunken. The hoof is completely twisted. The central groove of the frog is pushed together, leaving no room to physiologically widen. This hoof distortion has left a perfect recess in the frog for anaerobic bacteria (thrush).

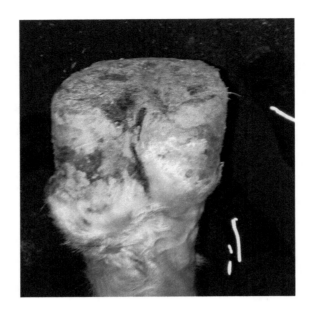

A few weeks later, after only one treatment, the hoof capsule was more relaxed. The tubules could now grow unhindered downward in the orientation they were supposed to.

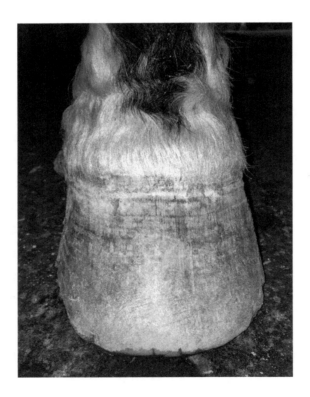

The coronet was much more even, no roof on the medial side, the tubules could grow down without being distracted. The wound was treated with medical honey, no more medication and the horse was not lame.

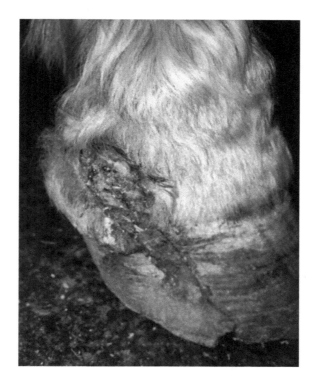

The wound healed nicely; the statics of the hoof were taken care of. The next picture shows the extent of the abscess eating away on the horn tubules and epidermal lamellae.

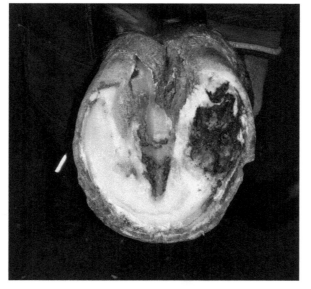

The macerated horn was trapped deeply under layers of double sole horn piled up for a long time on the horseshoe. The overall height of that hoof had to be reduced evenly, eliminating compression forces.

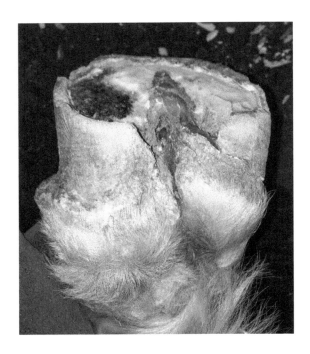

Three weeks after only one hoof treatment, the hoof shape had changed drastically. The central groove of the frog opened up, packing it with gauze (owner's homework) was important to apply stimuli for the corium to produce new horn.

It was clear that the heel wall would chip off, due to the extent of macerated horn in the lamellar layer. The bacteria had created a cavity, a disconnection of the hoof wall and the lamellae.

4 weeks later:

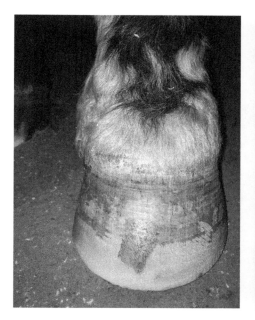 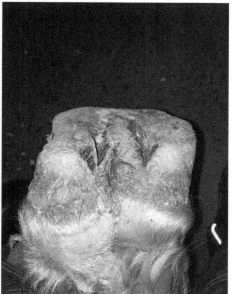

Although parts of the heel/quarter wall were missing, the horse had no problem as long as the 'horn shoe' was balanced. We see half an inch of a new horn growing down in new orientation (left picture above), indicated by a horizontal line.

Frog and medial heel were healing and new horn was produced:

The wound healed nicely; a new hoof wall grew down.

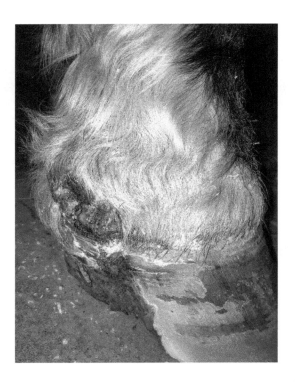

Another 4 weeks later, the wound had almost closed up.

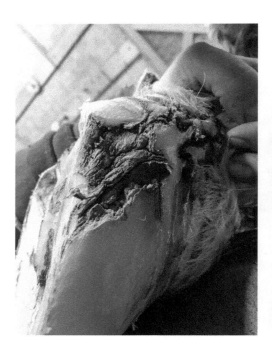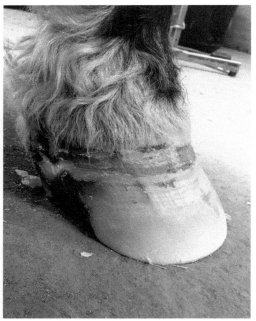

The old boy was doing great! He was back to work after the second treatment. The documentation stops here because very very sadly, he died of a severe colic a few weeks later.

Cracks

Nothing is so satisfying and easy to treat than hoof cracks. It is easy because the cracks themselves don't need to be addressed but rather the cause for them, i.e. the hoof shape. The cracks are just symptoms. They will automatically grow out when the hoof starts to rehabilitate and changes its shape. The time period for this can vary greatly, depending on existing hoof deformations. Most cracks and splits are completely gone after the renewal of the hoof capsule, which takes about 11 months. If the coffin bone and its hoof continue to remodel after a year or the horse is forced to change load on the limb due to accompanying factors (e.g., osteoarthritis, tendon damage), the process takes longer. Constant changes in the hoof capsule have an impact on the hoof mechanics, which must be permanently controlled by the hoof specialist. The crack cannot grow out if the hoof shape is not rehabilitated yet. If the hoof has concomitant circumstances like defects in the bone structure, crena, keratomas or horn scars, then the journey can become challenging and long-lasting but not impossible.

The pictures on the next page show clearly how the cracks grow out accordingly with the change of hoof shape. Not only flare causes cracks but it is surely one of the main causes. Cracks also appear on the more loaded, more used hoof side that might not have any flare or leverage.

Cracks happen when tubular and their intertubular horn are simply ripped out of their connection, they fan out due to levering forces. Once they are ripped apart, they cannot grow back together! The gap needs to grow out completely. The problem can start with lines that only appear in the outermost layer of the tubule horn in the hoof wall. Such a problem, caused by any kind of tension in the hoof capsule, is often resolved with a few filing treatments.

If those lines turn into cracks, they can cut through the complete hoof wall, often into the lamellar layer, leaving big gaps. In that case, the problem is more severe because now the hoof has two separated hoof wall sections acting against each other. Controlling those interacting forces is the main key to make the crack grow out. Cracks can also begin in the middle of the hoof wall or at the coronet. A clear sign of hoof distortion.

With the right treatment, the cracks will grow out with every millimeter of new hoof wall.

Example 1:

  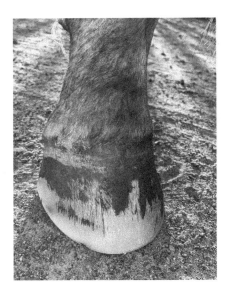

Example 2:

The arrows show the horizontal demarcation line that indicates where new hoof horn meets old hoof horn. The cracks end in that line, they never go above.

 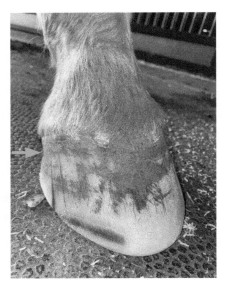 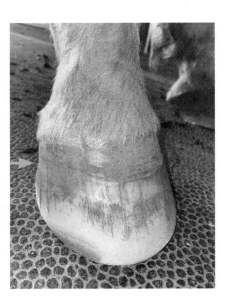

Some commonly used methods to stop cracks are often nonsensical and have negative effects on the hoof in the long term.

Very often a horizontal groove is cut into the hoof wall to 'stop' the crack. Unfortunately, nature cannot be tricked that easily. We see that the crack continues to act above the transverse groove. While the cause of the crack has not been eliminated, the levering sidewalls and the groove are then another new problem for the hoof. Once that groove grows down and reaches the ground, the already weakest part of the hoof capsule will be weakened even more. If not eliminated, the levers created by the flaring quarter walls will continue to pull the hoof into two halves. The hoof in the picture below has its natural abraded toe at the part of the hoof wall where the main crack is located. When the horizontal groove is close to the ground, that part will be weakened even more, strengthening the already too powerful quarter walls.

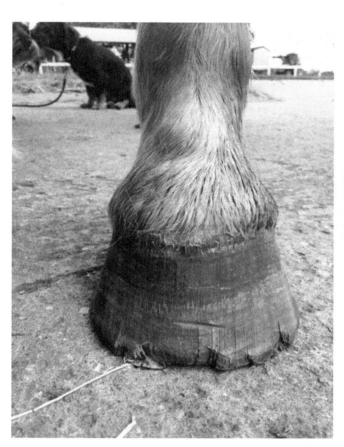

There is a similar problem observed with this foot:

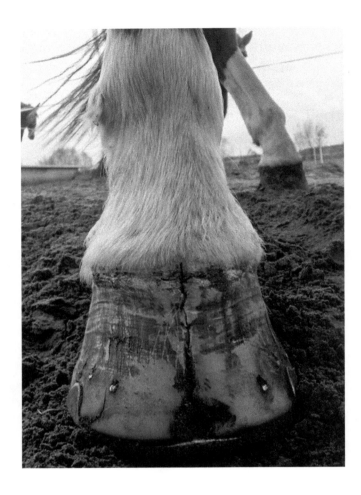

On the shoe, the natural abrasion is completely eliminated, causing the quarter walls to work deeply into the coronet. The two clips make that construct even stiffer and stronger. Ironically, they were applied to keep the quarter walls from flaring outward and to 'keep the crack together.'

Hoof physics work differently and cannot be tricked that easily.

Case 1

This poor draft horse not only had those cracks, he also suffered from mud fever and deep thrush on all four feet.

Right Fore Foot

Left Fore Foot

Despite the poor picture quality of the photo and dirty hooves, we can clearly see what causes the cracks. Now that your eye is trained more to recognize leverage and compression, it is visible how each hoof is being 'pulled apart' in the middle.

The lateral bulb of the right front (arrow) is pointy and pushed upward due to compression.

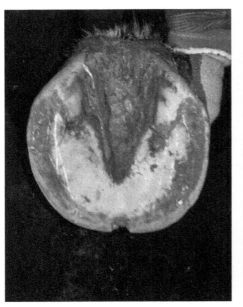
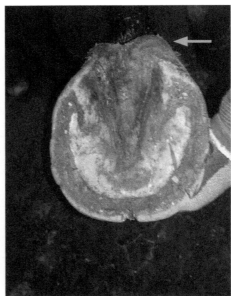

3 months later:

The hoof shape changes. Flare grows out but also compression forces disappear. The coronet is more balanced. The cracks go up to the leverage point, where the growth orientation of the tubules changes.

Another 3 months later:

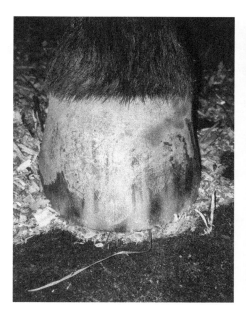 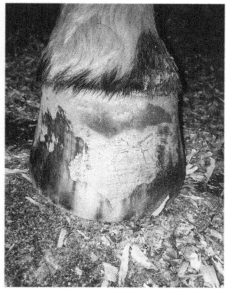

Everything is balanced, there is no thrush and even the pointy bulb looks more relaxed. Although the horse will always load that lateral heel mainly, it is mandatory to at least make the hoof as comfortable as possible. The horse lived with these feet for 26 years. At least for the remaining couple of years the old guy has left in life, he will walk in nice 'shoes'.

Left Fore   Right Fore

Case 2

The owner was told that these cracks are only superficial, caused by fungus. After trying all kinds of fungus treatment the economy has to offer without result, she introduced the horse to me and learned that there is no such thing as fungus on a hoof. I acknowledge such a thing as anaerobic fusobacteria, but not in this case. Again, in her horse's case, the focus was set on the symptom rather than the real cause.

The feet were completely out of balance. We can see how the hooves desperately try to grow down smaller and also steeper:

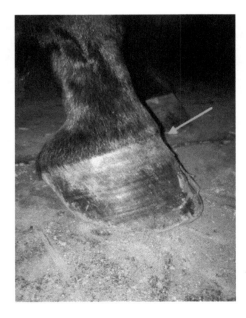

The arrow shows the kinked hoof wall tubules that try to grow down in a steeper orientation but are distracted.

2 months later:

With every millimeter of new horn, the affected tubules grow down as well. Fungus or bacteria would leave a destruction of wet macerated horn behind. In this case the tubules were dry and brittle because they were exposed to air.

4 months later:

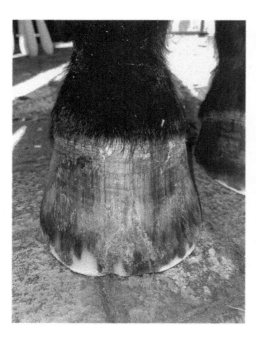 

7 months later:

The cracks will completely disappear in the next months.

This case can be followed on **www.hoofphysics.com**

Case 3

Left front hoof

 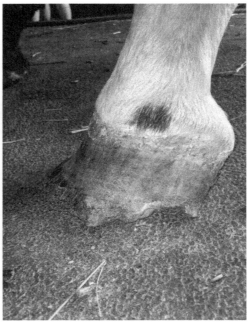

Leverage pulls the hoof apart. The hoof cracks in the middle of the toe, at the break over point. The quarter walls start bending after the first inch of growth. It is obvious that only changing the hoof shape will make the crack grow out.

2 months later:

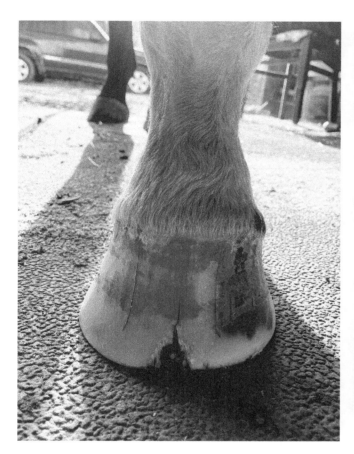 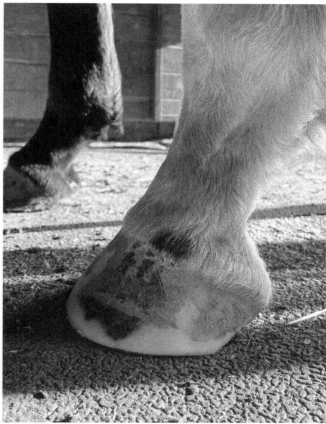

The hoof wants to grow out much smaller and steeper. The lateral view shows a deep horizontal indication line in the lower third, very well visible. Comparing dorsal and lateral view shows that the crack goes up until that exact line. The line demarks the greatest flare below the line, the part that is exposed most to leverage.

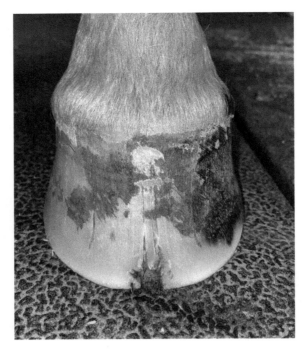

The hoof has grown out half way. The crack cannot grow out as long as the hoof walls are bent. We do see how straight the first half of the hoof grew out. The coronet is balanced. The horse will get a completely new hoof.

This case can be followed on **www.hoofphysics.com**

Laminitis

Laminitis is an inflammation of the dermal lamellae, which can lead to a disconnection of the coffin bone to its inner hoof wall, and actually the most controversially discussed hoof disease. While there is an agreement on the causes, the rehabilitation process is approached in very different ways. This occurs due to contradictory ideas about the physical processes taking place within a laminitic hoof after the initial acute phase is over.

Certain enzymes (matrix metalloproteinases) regulate a controlled detachment and reforming of cell compounds in a healthy hoof. This guarantees that the horn shoe can grow down while being firmly attached to the bone. Dermal lamellae and the epidermal lamellae create a strong bond through a connective tissue consisting of collagen, the basement membrane.

Excessive activation of these enzymes causes a breakdown of the basement membrane. This can be triggered by endotoxins but also endogenous messenger substances, as they are released by the body in the case of a severe general illness or stress. In other words, any extraordinary strain to the horse's metabolism could result in systemic laminitis.

Judging from my own observations, hormonal/endocrine pathologies such as Equine Metabolic Syndrome (EMS) and Pituitary Pars Intermedia Dysfunction (Cushing's Disease) have increased rapidly in the past years. They have become the main cause for laminitis cases.

As in any other disease, the real trigger must be recognized and treated in order to help the patient. It is useless to focus on hoof treatment if the cause of the problem is not identified and addressed. To ensure long-lasting hoof health, it is even more important to identify the type of laminitis.

The horse owner must be made aware of whether the animal requires a completely new diet and living conditions in the long run or whether the episode of laminitis is the short-term result of an event such as poisoning.

The diagnosis of the cause is also important for the initial measures in an acute diagnosed laminitis episode to interrupt the causal chain. Patients suffering from hormonal Laminitis (EMS, Cushing's) do not respond well to nonsteroidal anti-inflammatory drugs (NSAIDs) like Phenylbutazone. In hormonal laminitis, the destruction of tissue caused by inflammation is less severe than in toxic laminitis.

What Happens in the Hoof?

The causes can vary, but the result is the same. The suspensory apparatus of the hoof loses its functionality because the lamellae are being compromised. The bearing edge is the most accessible weight-bearing structure in the hoof. Physical forces reach and influence it first and are then transmitted to the inner parts. If the compromised connective tissue cannot withstand these forces, it will be unable to keep the hoof wall connected to the suspended coffin bone.

The hoof wall continues to deviate from the bone, especially the parts of the hoof wall that are already bent concavely to the ground. The thick dorsal hoof wall is exposed to the most leverage and therefore affected the most.

Without the coffin bone attached adequately to its protective hoof wall, the bone may sink into the capsule if support is lacking. The weight of the horse drives the bone down, the horn capsule gives way, and the bone sinks closer to the ground. The coffin bone can even break through the sole if the lack of support is severe enough. As long as the bearing edge has to carry any weight, there can be no support for the coffin bone in acute laminitis.

The sole penetration is then explained as a consequence of the course of the disease instead of as the cause of wrong treatment. If the correct hoof treatment is not provided, the damage to the suspensory apparatus can become chronic.

Any hoof support attached to the bearing edge will inevitably prolong the healing process or make it impossible altogether. No matter what kind of hoof protection is chosen, as long as the bearing edge touches the ground first, all tensile forces will act on the hoof wall first. The coffin bone will not have any support.

Even if an attempt is made to cushion the bone in addition to that fixed protection, the weight is still on the bearing edge first. This inevitably leads to further stress on the suspensory apparatus, which will be compromised even more. The active leverage leads to chronic changes in the dermal and epidermal lamellae.

The suspensory apparatus can only come to rest and regenerate itself if the load is taken off the bearing edge completely and the coffin bone is properly cushioned. Specially applied hoof pads can help achieve this, which a professional can easily make with cotton and duct tape. Correct handling is what counts, not how expensive the material is.

Without the bearing edge being loaded, the newly formed hoof wall horn can then grow down in the correct orientation, parallel to the bone and connected through intact lamellae.

It can do so because it is not being distracted in its orientation of growth. There is no unhealthy pressure and no tensile force changing the direction of growth while it is being produced.

After approximately 11 months, the hoof can be restored if suitable measures have been taken immediately from the beginning.

One crucial diagnostic measure in laminitis is the taking of x-rays. However, if these radiographs are being misinterpreted, the healing approach can differ immensely and even harm the horse.

Radiology is used to find out whether the bone has changed its position within the hoof capsule.

The focus lies on the deviation of the hoof wall and coffin bone. The first question should be if there is an actual separation between bone and hoof capsule caused by systemic laminitis or a deviation of the hoof wall caused mechanically by improper hoof care. In either cases, it is now up to the physical understanding of the individual professional to choose the right measures for healing.

In many scenarios, cause and effect are often confused and the real processes are not identified. The so-called 'coffin bone rotation' is determined to be causative for hoof wall and coffin bone deviation, meaning the coffin bone rotates backwards in the coffin joint into flexion. The rotation's cause is said to be the Deep Digital Flexor Tendon (DDFT), the strongest tendon connected to the coffin bone, which causes tension and therefore pulls the coffin bone into a flexion. It can supposedly do this because it lacks a counterpart that would prevent the tension and flexion. I don't agree with this supposition.

The DDFT is the main tendon responsible for bending the coffin bone in the coffin joint when the foot leaves the ground, therefore stretches most in midstance and at the moment of break-over when the weight passes over the toe and the heel begins to lift.

Its opponent is the Common Extensor Tendon (CDET), whose main task is to straighten the bent limb again and guide it forward for the movement.

Although the CDET has less tensile force than the stronger DDFT, it is considered a worthy opponent because it joins forces with the branches of the suspensory ligament that run forward around the fetlock bone and connect with the extensor tendon just above the pastern joint.

This clever anatomical construct prevents the coffin bone from rotating backwards under load. A horse with acute laminitis shifts its weight backwards on the heels as the hind legs take over most of the support. It stretches the front legs out to avoid the pressure and tensile forces of the painful toe. In this position, the DDFT does not have the most tensile force. Nature comes to the rescue and finds an excellent way to help itself; the horse always tries to find the best posture to have best protection from pain and save the internal structures.

Since the horse stands on its hoof capsule and not on the bone itself, all forces are first transferred to the hoof capsule. It is much more logical that the hoof capsule will move away from the bone due to these leverage forces in the event of a separation of bone and hoof wall.

Therefore, the term hoof capsule rotation is more appropriate than the term 'coffin bone rotation', a major difference. Is the term so important? Yes, it is. It evokes certain images in our head, a certain image of what processes are happening. If we have the image in mind that the horn shoe is moving away from the bone and not the other way around, the starting point for therapy is completely different. It has a significant impact on the horse's recovery and future functionality. For 25 years, I have had to experience over and over how horses have been disabled forever due to wrong approaches to healing.

Flexor tendons have been cut (tenotomy/desmotomy) in order to decrease the tension by tendon lengthening or the opposite: heels were artificially raised to decrease tension, which rather results in a contraction of the tendon in the long term. In this event, a real flexion in the coffin bone will be the result. Both approaches are very contradictory in my eyes and are not treating the actual cause: the deformation of the hoof capsule.

It is the detachment of the coffin bone from its foundation and the weight of the horse making the bone column sink closer to the ground that can and should easily be corrected by taking the bearing edge out of the load and letting the new growing horn reattach to its horn shoe at the origin of production, the coronet.

The two radiographs below of different horses show a separation of hoof wall and coffin bone and a distorted hoof wall. Both horses were diagnosed with coffin bone rotation.

The left picture shows a hyperextended hoof-pastern axis. How is a rotation possible in that case?

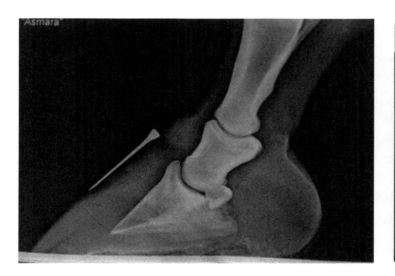 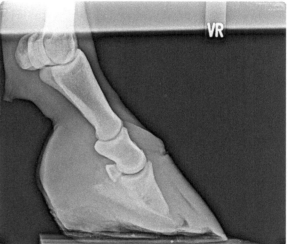

In the right picture, the coffin bone shows a flexion in its coffin joint. Look at the heel line of that hoof. It is parallel to the parietal surface of the coffin bone. This horse always had a broken forward hoof-pastern axis. The bone did not rotate, but the dorsal hoof wall did. It has lost ground height due to the divergence; therefore, the coffin bone lost its original position in the hoof capsule, and the weight of the horse pushes it closer to the ground. That can only happen when the weight is not being taken off the bearing edge.

This little pony had two very steep feet with a natural flexion in the coffin joint:

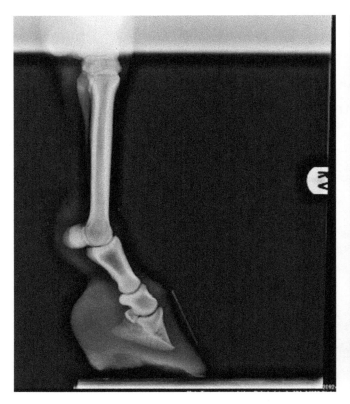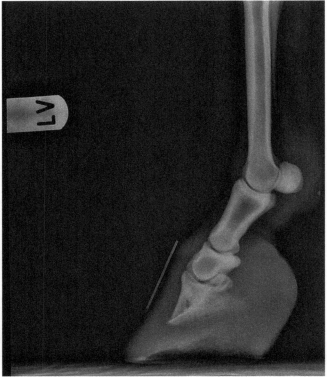

It was lame and shifted its weight back onto the hind feet. It clearly did not want to use the front feet. It was diagnosed with laminitis and coffin bone rotation.

The owner contacted me for consultation. I told her there was no acute laminitis to be seen on the x-rays, no separation between bone and hoof wall. But no doubt, the toe must have been very painful for the pony to use. The margin of the coffin bone showed deformation, the so-called lipping, due to the prevailing tensile forces the flaring toe had caused for years. The margin is slightly bent like a duck bill.

The pony was walking as if on stilts. After I reduced the leverage in the toe wall and reduced the hoof's overall height, it felt much better. Accumulated sole horn and hoof wall length caused so much pressure and tensile forces on the hoof that the pony simply could not stand comfortably in its horn shoe anymore. Although it showed very similar symptoms to laminitis, the pain was caused only mechanically, by improper hoof care.

This horse was diagnosed with laminitis and coffin bone rotation.

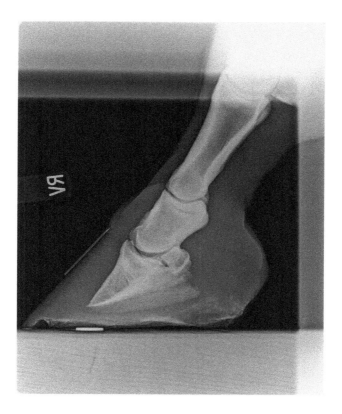

The hoof-pastern axis is aligned. The only thing rotated is the toe wall. The margin of the coffin bone shows lipping, it is deformed as a result of ongoing tensile forces as well. The toe wall has been pulled away from its coffin bone. Consequently, the lamellae are stretched, causing the margin of the coffin bone to remodel and adapt to the situation. The horse did not have a laminitis.

This horse has been diagnosed with acute laminitis, coffin bone rotation and was prescribed special shoes.

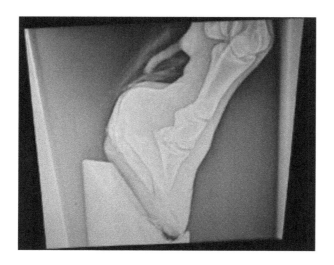

Not only is there no separation, but the laminitis also happened three months ago. You can see the newly produced horn already growing down underneath the coronet, perfectly aligned to the coffin bone in the first third of the toe wall and then distracted. The horse was lame due to an abscess.

To produce a meaningful x-ray image and to evaluate the hoof-pastern axis, certain criteria has to be observed.

The horse must fully load the limb, which is often difficult for the animal when the feet hurt!

The shape of the hoof needs to be taken into account when evaluating an x-ray. Do parts of the hoof wall already lever away, are they bent? Are there any x-rays for comparison? In almost all cases, no radiographs exist from the time before the laminitis happened.

Maybe the horse had a natural flexion in the coffin joint before the laminitis occurred?

The hoof pastern-axis can only be evaluated in a loaded condition. Radiographs such as the last one, where the hoof is positioned on a block, do not indicate the hoof-pastern axis or diagnose a 'coffin bone rotation'.

All hoof protection must be removed prior to radiographing, especially if the heels have been elevated. What sounds so obvious is unfortunately very often missed in practice.

Results of Wrong Hoof Treatment:

Wrong care of the hoof capsule after an episode of laminitis often leads to chronic damage of the suspensory apparatus or even the coffin bone.

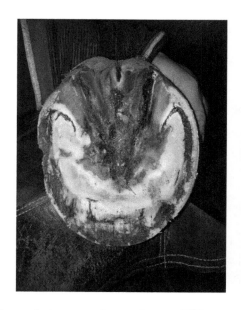 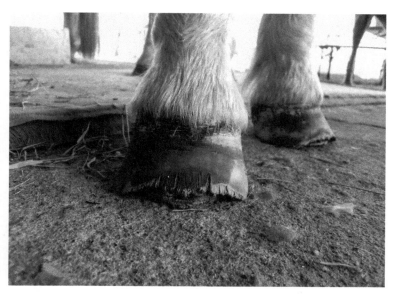

The pictures show two different horses. Both show an enlarged lamellar layer which acts as a wedge between the hoof wall and sole. After a laminitic episode, the dermal lamellae react with forming scar horn to repair the damage to the suspensory apparatus as quickly as possible. The produced epidermal lamellae are arranged in disarray, abnormally.

However, if the tensile forces of the hoof wall parts levering away are then not eliminated due to incorrect treatment, the scar horn cannot grow out. The suspensory apparatus cannot regenerate. The scar horn turns into a solid, dense horn wedge that drives the hoof wall further and further out. It distracts the hoof wall tubules in their physiological direction of growth. In addition, damage to the dermal lamellae and the coffin bone can occur, making the situation chronic. In many cases, it is still possible to restore the hoof completely, if the correct treatment is given. If the hoof has already been trapped in this chronic situation for years and there is chronic damage, the horse must and can live with the corresponding hoof situation. The hooves then need special attention. They have to be rasped at shorter intervals than healthy hooves in order to keep the deformation under control. Needless to say, this is only possible with a barefoot hoof exposed to natural abrasion.

Attempts to correct the deformed hooves with shoes in order to fix the 'coffin bone rotation' will inevitably fail.

With a shoe, the distracted hoof wall cannot be filed in the necessary short intervals. The lamellar wedge cannot be treated the right way and will cause further damage. The quarter walls will be overloaded in contrast to the levering toe wall. The horn tubules of the toe will fold, leading to the typical 'founder hoof'.

Removing the toe wall completely is another common measure in treating a laminitic hoof.

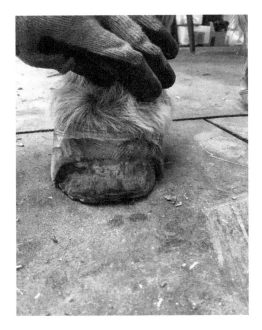

The removal of the hoof wall has negative effects on the overall statics of the hoof. In addition, it causes further damage to the lamellae in the long term.

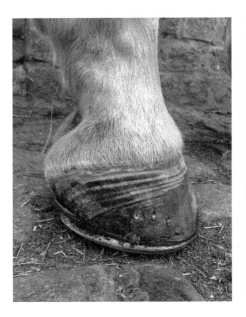

The hoof wall resection is unfortunately still a common measure in the correction of hooves affected by laminitis. It is not only counterproductive, but in some cases, it can even lead to the death sentence of the animal. Once the horse has survived the initial laminitis attack, the hoof reacts with repair measures.

This newly formed scar horn is perceived by many professionals as disturbing since it deflects the hoof wall like a wedge and allegedly contributes to the animal's perception of pain. To eliminate this deflection, the entire toe wall is removed, and the already damaged epidermal lamellae are exposed. They will dry out and cause further mechanical damage to the already stressed dermal lamellae. A vicious cycle begins. The path for chronic damage is paved.

The scar horn is a clever repair measure of nature. It is produced after the laminitis episode to maintain the damaged connection between wall and bone. Laminitis affects the entire suspensory apparatus of the hoof, not only the toe part. If the toe wall is removed, the quarter walls will become completely overloaded. This has an enormous impact on the coronary dermis of the quarter walls. It can lead to the chronic displacement of the coronet.

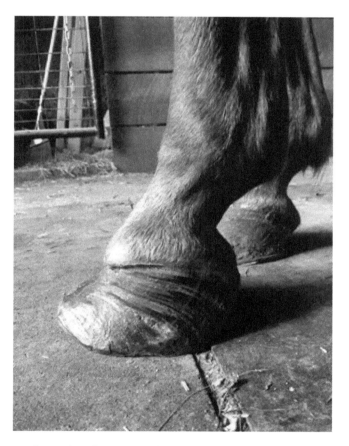

The coronet bulges up, then is displaced. The main weight rests on the quarter walls, and the toe wall has no function.

The toe wall urgently needs counter pressure to relieve the load of the quarter walls. It is important to shape the horn tubules in a way they can touch the ground, not to eliminate them completely. This is possible with the right rasping technique. The scar horn can easily grow out if given the chance. After 11 months, a laminitic hoof can completely recover if the right measures have been taken from the beginning.

As seen in the previous picture, these deformed hooves often appear higher in the heels, which is misinterpreted as increased growth in the heels. The height difference is simply created by the bent toe tubules and the resulting loss of height.

Often the heels are shortened without considering that the horse will undoubtedly react to this abrupt change negatively (section Club Foot).

Many barefoot trimmers see keeping the heels short as a panacea for various hoof problems. Especially in cases of laminitis, shortening the heels is advocated in order to help the laminitis hoof into its natural shape.

This can be very detrimental to the hoof. Excessive shortening of the heels puts immediate tension on the DDFT. The horse will react with muscle tension, which in turn will cause contraction of the tendon. This can cause the bone to shift backwards and to rotate over time.

The Effects of Shoes to Treat Laminitis

The x-rays show a hoof diagnosed with laminitis. The pictures show before and right after the 'corrective' measure.

Before   After

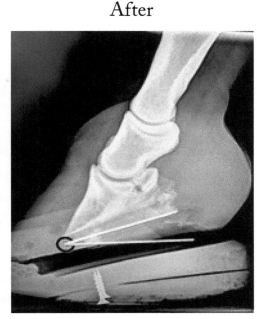

Before the shoe was applied, the bone axis showed a slight hyperextension in the pastern and coffin joint. After the 'correction', it is still slightly broken back in the pastern joint but now flexed in the coffin joint, exactly what needs to be avoided in a laminitic hoof.

The coffin bone has now been lifted more on its tip. Pressure is still acting on the bearing edge and will drive the toe wall further away from the coffin bone. The measure has not changed the natural heel angulation or height at all. The DDFT will have less stimuli and contract in the future, which will be almost impossible to reverse. The coffin joint is abruptly compressed and the navicular bone displaced.

Furthermore, this type of 'correction' does not improve the hoof wall and coffin bone discrepancy. On the contrary, the toe wall will now be driven away from the bone even more. As long as 'correcting' features are attached to the hoof wall, it will keep on bearing load, which causes permanent tensile forces and distract the new produced horn tubules and lamellae from their physiological growth direction.

Ongoing tensile forces will lead to chronic damage of the suspensory apparatus, not to mention the negative effects on other limb structures (osteoarthritis, joint deformities, bone modeling, bone lysis) due to the abruptly changed load situation in all joints.

As mentioned earlier, the correction of the scar horn, the modified terminal horn and the proper filing of the hoof capsule are essential to the correction of a laminitic hoof.

However, this is not possible with a shod horse. The shoe covers precisely those parts of the hoof that need to be corrected, in short intervals, at least every two weeks.

In the next case, the x-rays show how systematically, in a period of three years, the horn shoe has continued to change negatively, while the bone axis has remained the same. The toe wall was driven out further by the shoe. The modified epidermal lamellae together with the terminal horn were not corrected. The hoof is chronically damaged.

The change of position of the hoof-pastern axis results solely from the new unphysiological heel height, the way the horse is forced to use the limb. The toe is uncomfortable and so is the heel. That makes it hard for the horse to put weight on its limb at all.

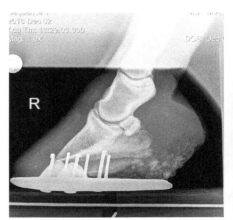 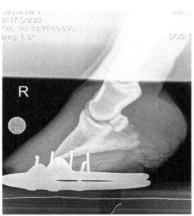 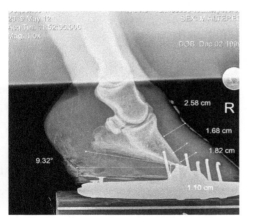

The result of chronically stretched epidermal lamellae and terminal horn can be seen in the picture on the next page. The lamellae seem to have merged with the sole horn to form a solid unit (arrow).

Notice how oval the hoof shape is due to the permanently driven forward toe. The bearing edge does not touch the ground; it cannot. The lamellar wedge is in the way, and the horse is forced to walk on it, which is painful.

3 months later:

The heels have opened up because they have less pressure due to the toe that immediately helped bear the weight after the removal of the shoes and correct trimming. The terminal horn and epidermal lamellae have been cut back systematically. The dorsal hoof wall reaches the ground. The horse can break over much easier. If the sensitive lamellae stay damaged and cannot produce functioning epidermal lamellae, the dorsal hoof wall will always stay bent.

Nevertheless, the best possible situation needs to be created; a comfortable horn shoe without further painful mechanics.

I understand that every professional aims to make the horse feel better immediately. Often the shoe is used because it acts as a painkiller. The hoof mechanics are restricted and the horse feels less pain. Unfortunately, however, associated negative hoof capsule deforming effects then set in, often only becoming visible months later. The horse owner must be clear about whether it is better to give the horse relief for the moment with the accompanying later chronic consequences or whether he lets the horse tolerate a few weeks of discomfort and achieve a fully restored hoof in the long term. Laminitis is a severe disease. It takes a full year for the horse to recover; we need to be aware of that. Often analgesics are administered at the same time as the shoe is applied. It is then necessary to assess exactly whether the hoof treatment or the administered remedy contributed to the improvement. What happens when the pain medication is discontinued? Often a new lameness sets in immediately.

My dear colleague and friend Anja Küchler, German hoof orthopedist and veterinarian, kindly provided the following cases. She came across both of these in Austria. The treating veterinarian of both horses took the provided x-rays.

Both cases show how the application of shoes made the situation worse. In both horses, the coffin bones of both front hooves broke through the sole due to incorrect hoof management.

Case 1

Left fore foot

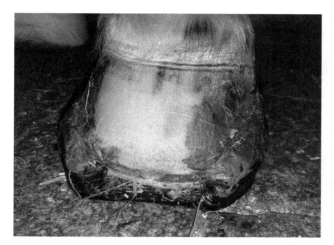 

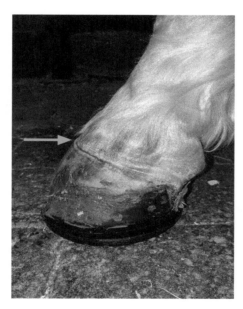

The laminitis episode happened three months ago. In the third picture, we see the deep groove (arrow) in the hoof wall, kinked tubular horn from when the initial episode happened. Since the pressure has not been removed from the bearing edge and is still acting on the hoof walls, the horn tubules are deflected in their vertical alignment at the origin of production. The papillae that produce the tubular horn are inevitably pushed horizontally during an acute laminitis episode. Due to the lack of connection, the weight on the bone acts against the leverage of the toe wall, the horn producing papillae are bent and the papillae are forced to change their orientation, from vertical to horizontal. The horn tubules are kinked, a groove is created.

The problem with laminitis is that the acute phase goes unnoticed. Only when the horse starts feeling pain, due to the subsequent separation, can immediate action be taken. But then the destructive processes are already underway. They can only be stopped if the load is removed immediately from the bearing edge.

In this case, this did not happen. The bone had no support and caused it to sink even further. In addition, the heel was raised, which tilted the coffin bone even further onto its tip. The x-ray is not suitable for assessing the hoof-pastern axis, but one can clearly see how the coffin bone penetrates the sole. The newly produced hoof wall has no chance but to be deflected. It cannot grow down parallel to the coffin bone. It will keep on tearing at the suspensory apparatus and cause chronic damage.

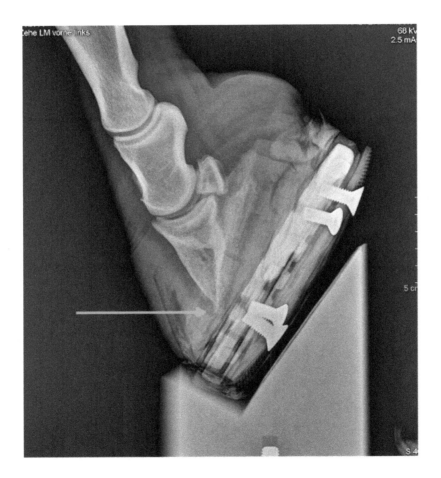

The x-ray shows how deep the bones are sunk into the hoof capsule. They had no support. The newly produced hoof wall had no chance to connect with its coffin bone. The arrow shows a bent coffin bone margin.

2 months after Anja started her hoof treatment:

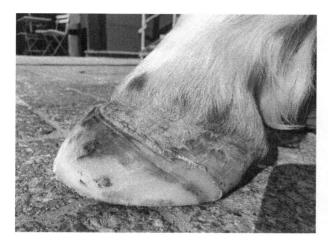 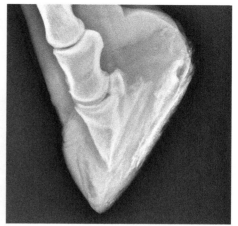

New horn growth in new orientation is seen in the first inch of the hoof wall below the coronet. The x-ray shows exactly the same thing. The horse walks better. The tip of the bone is still close to the sole, but the new connected hoof wall hinders it from breaking through because Anja took the load from the bearing edge. Instead, the coffin bone is being supported with special cushions. The gap in the sole can close and the bone is protected:

In the past, cases with sole penetration were thought to be the death sentence for the horse. But we know that it is possible to heal the hoof again if we give it time to grow back.

8 months later:

Ongoing metabolic issues and associated abscess left their marks in the hoof wall.

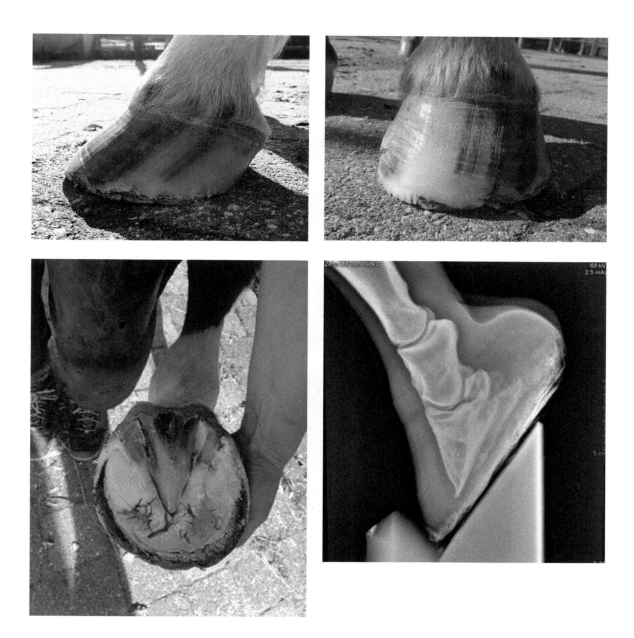

The situation has much improved. The chronically changed epidermal lamellae will always slightly deflect the hoof wall from the bone, but the horse feels comfortable.

Case 2

The next case shows similarly applied shoes with the same consequences.

Left Fore:

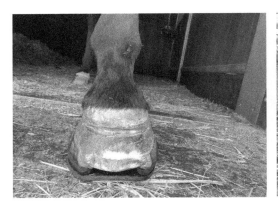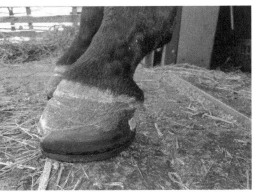

In addition to the shoe, a horizontal groove has been cut into the dorsal hoof wall, combined with a partial hoof wall resection. We discussed the negative effects of the shoe to the lamellae and the hoof statics earlier. In my opinion, it is a cruel and nonsensical procedure.

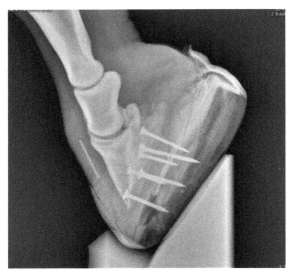

The laminitis happened five months ago.

The coffin bone has sunken deeply into the hoof capsule. Months after the laminitis happened, the horse still did not improve with the taken measures. The horse could barely walk. The green line shows the new hoof wall tubules trying to grow down alongside the coffin bone and then deflect. The deflected hoof wall part has been radically filed off, leaving the lamellae exposed (first picture, dorsal view). This measure was an attempt to adapt the hoof to the coffin bone visually, but instead, it has become utterly devoid of function.

With the shoe, the weight of the horse still weighs on the bearing edge. In addition, the quarter walls are overloaded because the toe was taken out of use. The coffin bone is no longer supported; it sinks into the hoof capsule.

A construction artificially attached from the outside cannot replace the actual organic functionality of the hoof capsule.

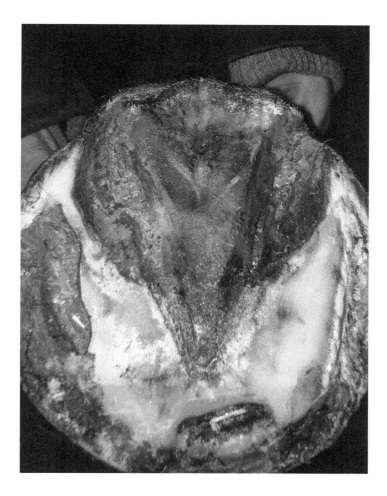

In this case as well, the coffin bone penetrated the sole.

Recovery started with Anja's treatment. The hoof capsule had to be restored completely new. A year later, the best possible situation was achieved.

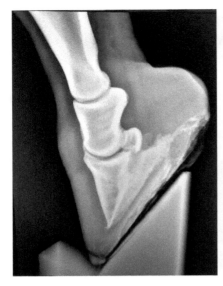
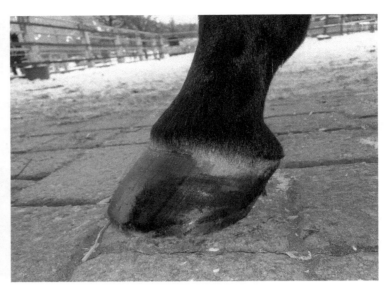

The lamellae stayed stretched, causing a slight deviation of the hoof wall from the coffin bone. As a result of that ongoing stretch, the margin of the coffin bone remodeled.

The horse is sound and is being ridden.

I would like to emphasize once again that any abrupt change in hoof shape is problematic for the horse. It influences the horse's control of balance. Every abrupt change must be compensated with different muscle movement of the particular limb. The nervous system in the adult horse is already used to a certain hoof shape. The slightest abrupt changes will give new information to the musculoskeletal system during landing and toeing off and influence the horse's balance. In other words, the horse needs to learn how to walk anew every time we change situations abruptly.

Proponents of the shoe as a corrective measure for laminitis will be difficult to convince. However, the fact that a shod horse has no abrasion is indisputable.

Over the course of 20 years, my experience has been that no artificial 'aid' can regenerate a laminitic hoof as quickly as the barefoot itself, if exposed to abrasion and if prepared the correct way. Living conditions and the right nutrition play a major role for a horse that suffered from laminitis. Horses with metabolic predispositions such as EMS or PPID need to be monitored precisely. They tend to suffer from recurring laminitis episodes if their metabolic impairment is not brought under control. The best hoof care is ineffective if the trigger for the problem is not managed properly. That can be a considerable challenge for the owner. It takes a lot of homework to obtain the knowledge to keep the horses' disease under control. It is not enough to adjust the horse with medication.

Especially horses suffering from EMS usually need completely new living conditions.

A combination of the proper diet, herbs, homeopathy, strict exercise and hoof care can help these patients to a normal life. However, this requires a tremendous commitment from the horse owner and needs to be discussed with the attending veterinarian.

I mentioned Phenylbutazone (Bute) earlier. It is, besides other NSAIDs, the most popular prescribed medication for pain in horses in the United States. I do not want to deprive the animals in pain of their medication, but I recommend to please administer them responsibly. I had never seen so many over-medicated horses before I came to this country.

Phenylbutazone is very effective but also has the greatest side effects, which is why it was banned in Germany for horses for many years. The pamphlet warns of side effects, including gastro internal ulceration, kidney damage and internal bleeding, especially in ill or stressed horses, if overdosed.

In the past years, the sick horses I was introduced to already were adjusted to Phenylbutazone or other NSAIDs over months, in one case until even 1.5 years. That is what I call an unnecessary over-medication! Phenylbutazone can also falsely decrease thyroid hormone levels and give a false diagnose about Hypothyroidism, often mixed up with EMS. So how can a horse suffering from laminitis caused by an impaired metabolism recover if the metabolism is continuously burdened and intoxicated by overly-used medication?

For the last three years, I have seen Bute cans sitting on the shelf right beside the first aid kid or the horse grooming box, being fed like candy whenever the horse had an "ouchie." It is a prescription drug and should be used responsibly! The enormous side effects of any NSAID administered are very much underestimated, although they are very often the reason why a horse cannot recover from the initial laminitis episode.

In these three years, I have seen four horses die of side effects from painkillers instead of dying of the initial disease. This is unnecessary. There are so many alternative approaches to really solve the problem. A more effective long-term solution without side effects is based on the right diet, herbs, antioxidant supplements containing plant-based sources. Blood flow support in the hoof through herbs and providing the proper hoof care is mandatory.

Besides, pain is a natural protection measure of the body. A horse that suffers from laminitis should NOT walk around, not in the first phase of an episode. Later, yes, when the hoof starts to recover and the new connected hoof wall grows down.

Eliminating the pain will motivate it to walk even more and harm the suspensory apparatus. Of course, the pain must be controlled but not eliminated. If the pain becomes too much, the horse will know what to do and eventually lie down more, which is encouraged! If the horse could sit on the couch and put up its hurting feet all day, there would be no hoof problems due to laminitis! It is the weight of the horse and the permanent load on the hoof that cause the problems.

If the correct measures are taken right away, it is much easier to restore a hoof completely.

The pony in the next case had the laminitis episode in June 2020. The owner got referred to me, and together with the vet, the right measures were taken. I was not comfortable with the Bute and instead suggested a homeopathic remedy to increase blood circulation and reduce pain, in agreement with the veterinarian. The pony was tested positive for EMS. The owner started the proper diet right away.

The x-ray images were taken prior to my first visit. The hooves show an aligned hoof-pastern axis at the time the laminitis happened.

The hoof wall of both hooves already flared in the toe, which was never addressed before. The hooves showed the flare already before the laminitis, and such a deformation does not happen overnight. The margin of the coffin bone shows a slight lipping already, the first signs of remodeling and a certain proof that tensile forces were ongoing for a long time already.

The lamellae were stretched but hard like a wedge, which also develops in the long term and does not happen overnight.

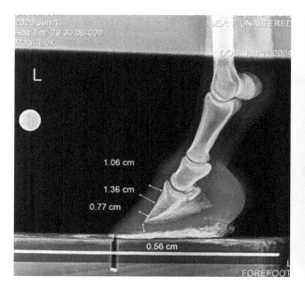 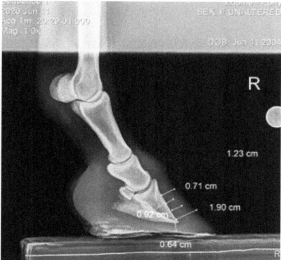

The hoof viewed from outside showed exactly the same signs. A flaring toe wall.

 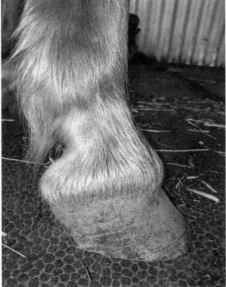

The little girl was pain-free very quickly. The laminitis was caught early enough.

September:

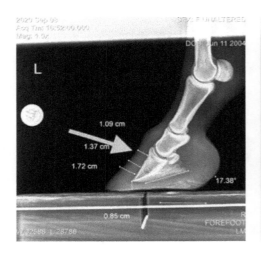 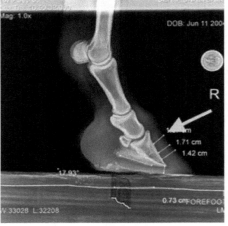

The new hoof horn grows out parallel to its coffin bone. The arrows mark the point where the orientation of the hoof wall tubules changes.

October:

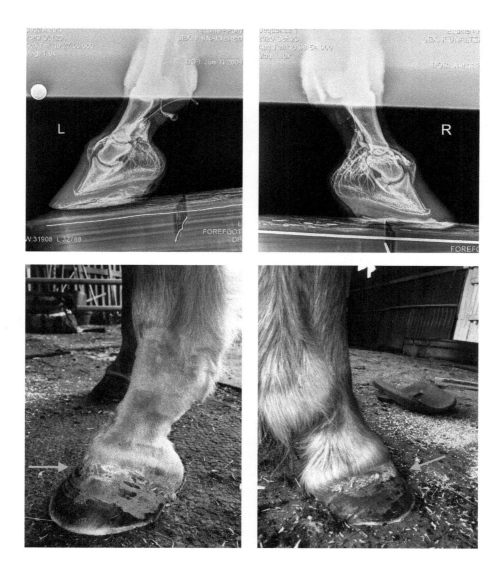

Another month later, the flare has grown out a bit more.

The owner still had to find the right solution and adjustment for the metabolic deficiency. In October, the mare had problems again, which were quickly taken care of by owner and vet. Poor girl had to have a new diet – even though she liked eating so much.

Half a year later, the hoof wall still deviates but the situation has improved. It can clearly be observed that there is no such thing as a coffin bone rotation happening in laminitis. Preparing the horn shoe determines the relation between the inner and the outer line.

April 2021:

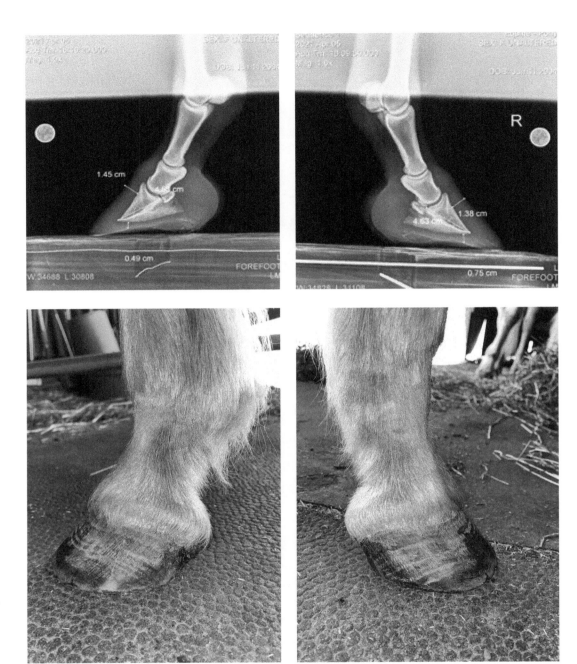

The lamellae are still stretched, the rehabilitation process is ongoing. It has not even been a year since these last pictures were taken. I expect much more improvement with continued treatment.

This case can be followed on **www.hoofphysics.com**

The laminitis in the next case happened six months before the picture was taken. It shows how the new horn grows down straighter, still distracted due to the old lever but already in a new orientation.

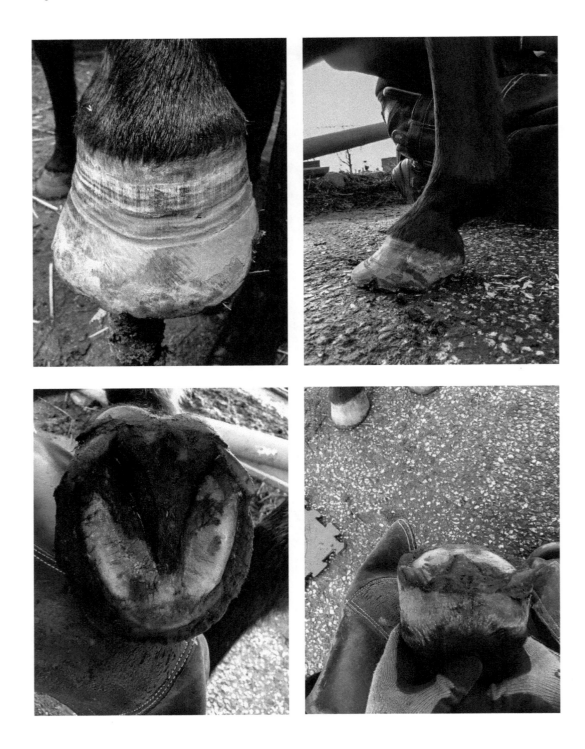

8 months:

 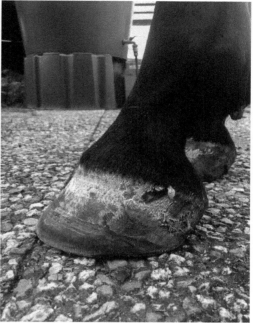

11 months:

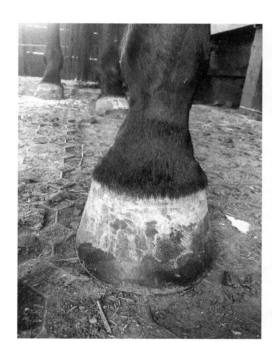 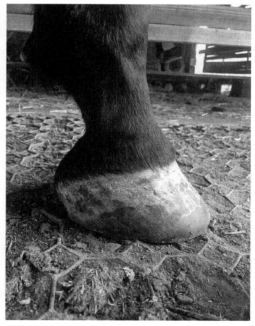

Keratoma

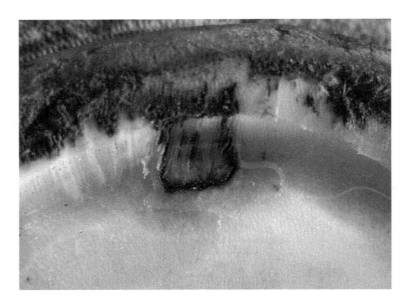

The image shows a circular widening of the lamellar layer known as the keratoma. In English-speaking countries, this keratinized horn structure is defined as a benign tumor. In Germany, this phenomenon is called 'Hornsäule', literally translated as a 'horn column', and is in no way compared with a tumor. Although the terminology varies, there is agreement on the treatment and the causal chain. The keratin mass is considered the cause of bone resorption and hoof wall deformities.

The degenerative lamellar layer between the coffin bone and the hoof wall grows abnormally. It is filled with proliferated keratinized tissue which applies pressure on the coffin bone and the hoof wall.

I don't agree with that.

 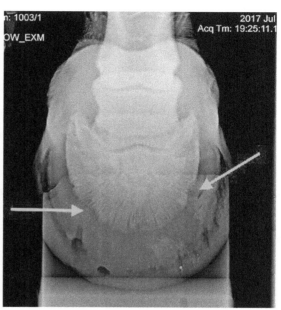

What if it is the other way around? And why are keratomas located exactly in those areas of the hoof that suffer most from pressure and tensile stress? Coincidence? As we know, bone tissue reacts to precisely those negative permanent forces with remodeling processes. It is not uncommon to find bone lysis, little notches as shown on the x-ray, at the coffin bone's distal margin, or at other spots in the coffin bone. Chronic irritation and stress to the dermis that covers the bone due to hoof imbalance can cause bone resorption.

If the bone has a defect, the dermis covering the bone must inevitably adapt to these changes. However, the hoof wall horn tubules are produced normally and grow down in their normal orientation. A distance is created, and a gap between the hoof wall and defective coffin bone must be filled. The dermis responds with increased horn production to fill this gap: the keratoma. It is nothing more than filling material, not a tumor.

Unfortunately, the replacement material is an inferior horn product, susceptible to pathogens. Abscesses can develop.

If the keratoma is now considered the trigger for bone resorption, the treatment approach taken is quite different. The tumor has to come out. In order to completely eliminate the keratoma, parts of the hoof wall are often removed. This surgical measure is not infrequently recommended, especially in connection with an emerging lameness. However, the question arises as to whether the lameness comes from the keratoma or is caused by the unfavorable hoof shape, which permanently irritates the dermis?

In my opinion, the surgical approach makes absolutely no sense. The missing bone substance will not fill up, which means the interstitial space, as a result, will not disappear. The dermis will always react with increased horn production to repair the gap.

I have treated a lot of horses with keratoma over the past twenty years. Most of the clients were not aware that their horse had a keratoma. They were never discovered because they usually do not cause any problems for the horse. They only become problematic when the tensile and pressure forces are not eliminated at the corresponding section of the hoof, and the affected dermis becomes even more affected. If the gap gets larger due to leverage forces, this in turn provides excellent entry points for bacteria (see section Abscess). Viewed from a different perspective, the logical approach of the hoof specialist is simpler... bring the hoof capsule into balance and eliminate any factors that further bone lysis.

When surgery is executed, the owner and horse are left alone afterwards with the result:

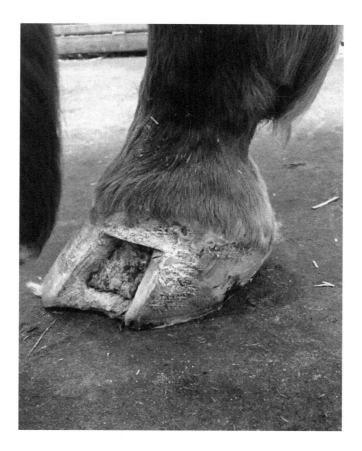

The trimmer/farrier who did the work before surgery can now deal with the compromised, completely inoperative hoof capsule. The separated hoof wall parts will now work against each other, increasing leverage due to tensile forces, making the actual problem worse.

High/Low Syndrome and Club Foot

The desire to adjust differently-angled forelimbs is a hopeless mission for many hoof trimmers.

The effort to achieve an optical adaptation of both hooves often exceeds the physiological potential of the horse's musculoskeletal system.

Many horses that were presented to me over the past 20 years have suffered irreparable damage from these corrective measures - mainly from the systematic shortening of the heels.

I agree that there are disadvantages resulting from a differently-angled toe axis and the negative impact on the horse's biomechanics. In stance, the horse will favor the more comfortable, lower foot. The different heel height results in different positions of the shoulder blade which has an impact on the horse's musculoskeletal system.

This resulting asymmetry has an effect on the horse's movement. However, the horse does not usually have any severe problems at all with this situation, which was adapted to at an early age. It is only when we try to demand more from the animal than its physical constitution is capable of that the problems begin. Why do we want to turn a horse with unequal limbs into a high-performance athlete? And why was the problem not addressed immediately after birth with a corresponding prospect of success (surgically or through hoof correction)? After the age of only six months, it is often too late to eliminate muscle contractions and the associated shortening of the tendons by corrective trimming measures like repeated shortening of the heels. One result of this measure is compensatory actions by the horse to avoid pain and inevitable changes in the hoof capsule or even bone remodeling.

When is a Hoof too High?

Experts have different opinions about the degree of the palmar angle of the coffin bone or its toe angle. In the meantime, there is a general consensus that anything steeper than 55 degrees on the toe wall is 'abnormal' and unsound. The heels must be lowered!

Often, however, no distinction is made whether the entire toe axis has a steeper angle overall or whether there is flexion in the coffin joint.

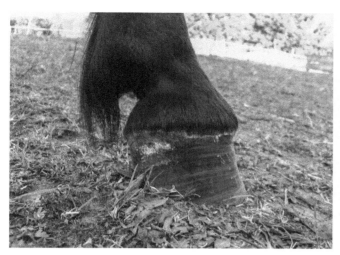

Hoof with flexion in coffin joint

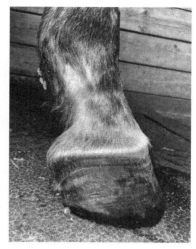

High heel, steep but aligned
hoof-pastern-axis

Both examples in the pictures above have a parallel hoof with a flat pastern bone and flat heel.

The hoof trimmer often does not differentiate between the two problems. In general, the higher hoof is considered the abnormal one, and the heels are shortened. In the first case (picture on the left), one hopes for an alignment of the toe axis (making the hoof match with the pastern angle). In the second case, one hopes that the shortening of the heel will result in an overall flattening of the entire hoof-pastern axis, which is already aligned. A higher heel height in this case is imperative for the hoof's steeper pastern bones.

A permanent lowering is not possible in both cases. The adult horse is not able to stretch tendons or muscles with long-lasting results. In contrast, with every abrupt effort, the muscles will continue to contract due to unpleasant stimuli and keep trying to return to their original state (height). The more we try to change the adapted form radically, the more we achieve the opposite. Continuous attempts, regardless of the short trimming intervals, will not keep the hoof down. The horse will try to grow to its physiological heel height again and again between the intervals.

It is even possible that high hooves become even higher over time as a result of this treatment and that the coffin bone rotates even further back due to the contraction of the irritated muscles. In this case, an actual coffin bone rotation is created by man.

Despite the knowledge of neuromuscular relationships, the specialist literature still recommends shortening the heels.

Effects of these treatments are then explained as the typical problems, resulting from the 'unhealthy' constitution of the club foot. Instead, it is the treatment itself that causes the club foot to develop the problems.

Effects on the Hoof from Incorrect Treatment

Case 1

Case 2

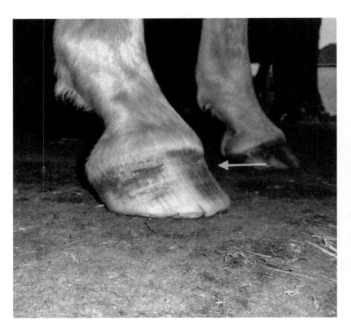 

Trying to keep the heels low will inevitably lead to bending of the toe wall. Both examples in the images show that the toe wall tries to grow down steeper than the heel angle. The heel was cut short systematically in the past. It doesn't matter if there is already flexion in the coffin joint or the complete hoof-pastern axis is steep overall. The bones, suspended in the tendons and their muscles, will not 'move' simultaneously with the trimmed hoof capsule shape. Only the suspensory apparatus of the hoof, in which the coffin bone is suspended, will be further stressed by this treatment because the hoof capsule will move away from the position of the coffin bone:

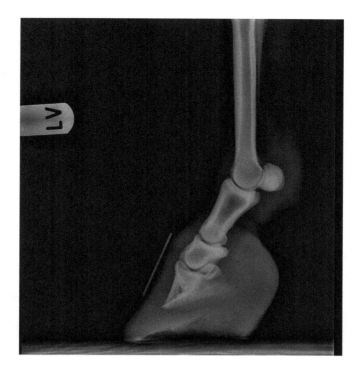

The coffin bone does not leave its position if the hoof capsule is manipulated.

The Deep Digital Flexor Tendon will experience more traction due to muscle contraction and will put more stress on the connective tissue of the coffin bone and the hoof wall in the toe area. The lamellae will be stretched, the hoof wall will be bent concavely, and it may lose ground height. The horse will then adjust to this situation, feeling uncomfortable. If the toe wall remains bent, the lamellae will continuously be stressed.

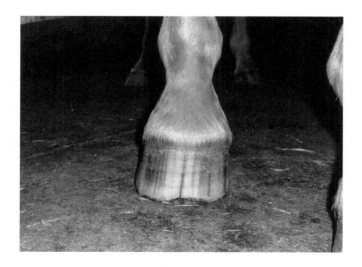

The dorsal view shows the already existing loss of height of the hoof wall in the middle of the toe due to the concavity of the wall. A crack has developed in the middle, starting in the part of the natural abraded toe. The tubules are torn apart and the toe wall splits exactly where most of the pressure is generated during toe lifting.

Solar view:

Case 1

Case 2

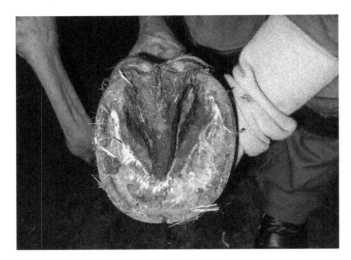 

The lamellar layer is stretched at the toe in both cases. The permanent concaveness of the toe wall and the associated leverage can result in bone remodeling:

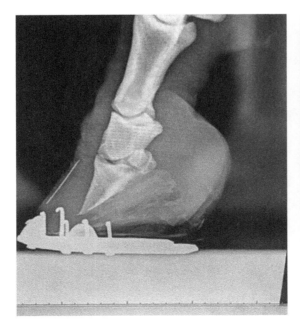 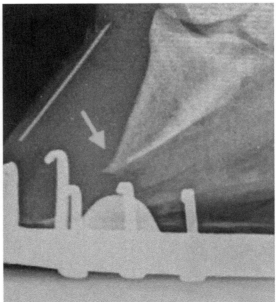

The distal margin of the coffin bone shows lipping, it is bent upwards, due to the continuous tensile forces. This can also lead to bone lysis.

Professionals explain the appearance of 'growth rings' in the toe wall claiming that the hoof wall horn is growing increasingly in the heel compared to the toe and therefore the heel needs to be shortened. I don't agree.

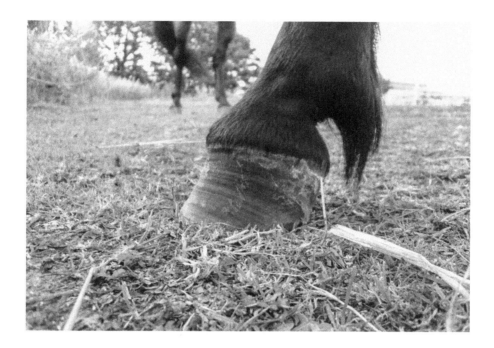

From a physical point of view, the problem is easy to explain and fix. Stop shortening the heels and address the concavity in the toe wall. The stress rings in the toe wall are a result of compression caused by a bending hoof wall. That's why they are more compressed in the front and divert in the heel. The tubule horn is simply folded and hindered in its direction of growth. The stress rings will disappear the moment the hoof regains its physiological shape.

In my opinion, all the negative side effects of a club hoof and its lack of functionality described in the specialist literature stem from incorrect treatment and not from the club hoof itself.

The horse in the next case covers pretty much all side effects of incorrect club foot treatments possible in only one hoof:

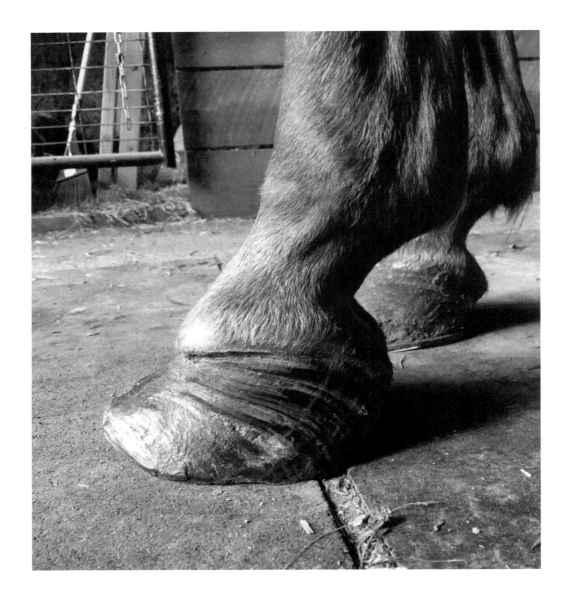

Having corrective shoes her whole life caused a terribly flaring and compressed toe wall. Permanent stress to the suspensory apparatus led to permanent damage of the dermal lamellae. A lamellar wedge was the result with similar symptoms as in a chronic laminitic hoof. The permanent tensile forces of the toe wall and the pressure of the lamellar wedge caused bone lysis. The horse suffered from recurring abscesses. The 3rd one just opened up by the time I first saw her. The loss of functionality of the toe wall caused the quarter walls to be overstressed. Dislocation of the coronary dermis, together with its subcutis, is the result (bulging).

4 months later:

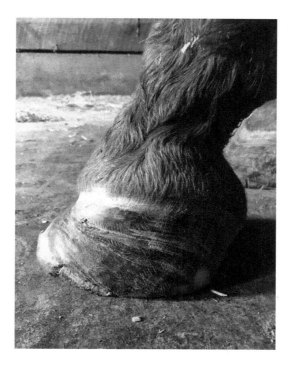

Today:

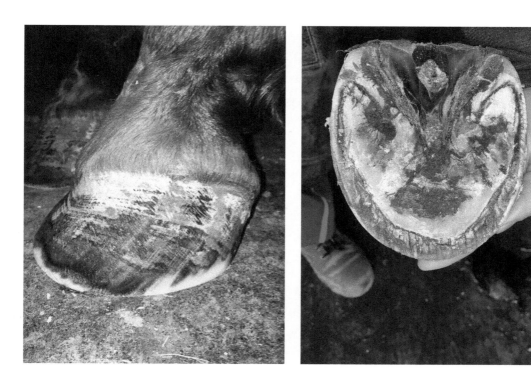

The damage done is irreversible. The dermal lamellae and resulting lamellar wedge will always cause a deflection of the hoof wall, causing an overstressed quarter wall.

Despite all that, the horse is not lame. She's jumping and running around like a maniac. If I take off a millimeter too much on the heel height, she will let me know the next day. The right expertise and experience to treat such a condition are mandatory.

With the right treatment and accompanied physiotherapy, a horse with such a 'disability' can have a perfectly pain free life. Maybe it is us who should think about not using our horses beyond their individual physical limits.

In the whole discussion about addressing the correction of the steeper hoof, the parallel flat hoof often remains neglected. Underrun heels are often considered a normal condition that cannot be corrected, so the focus is placed on the abnormal-looking foot. I, of course, have to disagree. It is essential to address the correction of the more loaded and often more deformed flat foot and also to achieve an approximation of the angulation of both feet by adjusting the foot that is too flat. Of course, that cannot be achieved with shoes. When the right treatments are applied, it is nice to see how quickly the collapsed heel of the flat hoof recovers. Suddenly, the steep hoof doesn't look so steep anymore!

Correction of Uneven Hoof Heights Starts at Foal Age, in the First Weeks and Months!

Stretching muscles and tendons is still possible at an early age (first six months) by controlling the heel height through trimming. At a later age, we can only accept the missed correction approach and its result.

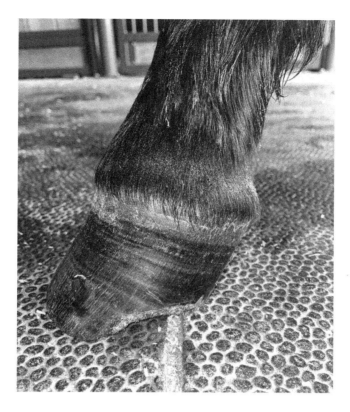

This little girl is only 10 months old but already shows a flare in the left front toe wall. The left hoof is smaller and higher than the right one which is rounder and flatter.

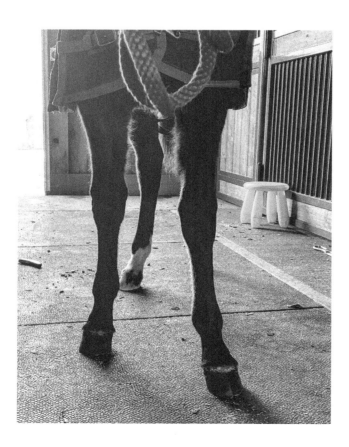

No matter how I move her back and forth, she always favors her right front, turns out the left foot and places it forward. Due to the additional flare, the left one has become even more uncomfortable for her to use.

Efforts to force the heels down by leaving the flare in the left front foot did not lead to any success. She will keep her slightly higher left foot, which is fine. At ten months old, it is already too late to make height correction through hoof care.

Cause and Effect

The desire for a 'symmetrical horse' is understandable. The effects of unequal limbs on the entire musculoskeletal system are undeniable. When a horse has reached an older age, it has to be considered whether possible movement anomalies are caused by a crooked foundation or if the hooves adapted in their shape to an already dysfunctional body structure.

The causes for the formation of an uneven foundation are developed at the foaling age. Acquired grazing patterns of the foal cause the limbs to be placed differently to the ground. If a foot is placed forward, it will reach the ground at a shallower angle than the limb placed backwards or more under the weight.

Favoring components will now add more load to the favored leg, which leads to further deformation in regard to the already existing angulation. The heels of the flat hoof will run under even more, and the retreating hoof will become steeper. The road to high-low syndrome is paved. Later, the rest of the body has to compensate for this imbalance. Appropriate corrective measures, as already explained, will not lead to improved well-being of the horse.

The development of an acquired broken forward hoof-pastern axis on only one foot can be caused by a variety of factors. Incorrect or excessive use of foal starters can lead to a growth imbalance between bones and tendons. Incorrect hoof trimming, the elimination or wrong care/assessment of the foal hoof crease and wrong living conditions all favor the development of the club foot.

As the owner of an adult horse with a club foot or unequal high hooves, it is important to accept the given situation. Very often, individual specialists, who of course all care about the animal's well-being, are happy to delegate the problem-solving. The horse trainer would like the horse to have equal hooves so that he/she can demand appropriate performance. The hoof trimmer would instead have adapted training, knowing that the hooves or the position of the limbs cannot ensure certain performance goals. These two perspectives usually put the horse owner in a bind. Instead of looking for the fault in only one place, it is now imperative that both sides work hand in hand. Correct hoof treatment also includes physiotherapy and adjusted training. Easier said than done when opinions about what is correct vary so much.

Hoof Wall Cavity/White Line Disease

Most professionals already agree that the term 'White Line Disease' is misleading and does not define the actual ongoing processes properly. The so-called 'disease' is neither a disease nor does it affect the white line at all in most cases. I don't know why experts still use that term. I also don't know why the originally called 'golden line' (due to its rather greyish golden color) all of a sudden was defined as 'white'. But I do know, ever since the word 'disease' was added to the already confusing terminology, the hoof product industry started booming.

Hoof pathogens such as fungus and bacteria were taken as the initial trigger for a then-persistent problem. Once again, cause and effect have been confused.

A lot of symptoms such as seedy toe, stretched epidermal lamellae maceration or separation of lamellae and hoof wall have been put under the umbrella of the term 'White Line Disease'. However, these are all completely different symptoms with a different cause and different treatment approach. For the hoof specialist, it is essential to use different terminologies to differentiate individual problems from one another. The individual problems only have one thing in common: they result from unfavorable mechanical forces due to unphysiological loading of the suspensory apparatus with subsequent bacterial infections. Once there is a gap or a weak connection, it makes it easy for the anaerobic bacteria to stick to the horn.

In order to understand the different causes, we need to be able to understand hoof physics.

A distinction must be made as to whether the golden line, together with the epidermal lamellar layer, are affected or if the lamellar layer alone is affected; or whether both are completely intact and a cavity is formed between the intact lamellar layer and the tubule horn of the hoof wall.

No worries, I will break that down for you!

This hoof combines all problems in one:

The hoof is obviously very asymmetrical. The main load is on the left side. The hoof wall and bar on that side are more vertically oriented. The lateral frog sulcus (right in the picture) is covered by horn, which leans like a roof over it. The same goes for the right bar, it lays on the sole horn. It seems to push the already rounded quarter wall further out.

Interestingly, the gravel and dirt are stuck on the left side of the hoof and not so much on the right. There is a reason for it.

The close-up view shows a complete intact lamellar layer (arrow) in normal size. However, the golden line is now pink. We can see the gravel is stuck deeply between the intact lamellar layer and the tubules of the hoof wall.

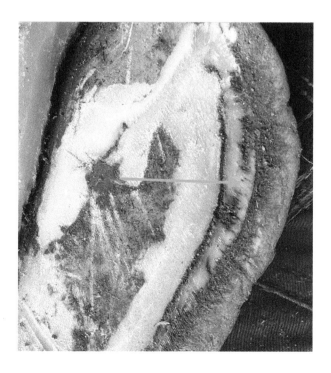

On the other side, there are no stones or dirt trapped. Instead, the area is closed and the lamellar layer looks completely different. It is stretched, its structure is hard to distinguish from the golden line. The entire area has a yellowish red color.

Different mechanical forces create different symptoms.

The hoof is more loaded on the left side. The weight of the horse pushes against the ground. The hoof capsule in between deforms. The less loaded part of the hoof has been pushed away from that center of load over the years. It was never corrected in the right way. The hoof stays loaded one-sided (left in the picture). Due to the load situation, all forces work proximally into the hoof on that side. The hoof wall cannot 'flee' to the side, bend or flare in that particular case. Due to load, shear forces work proximally. They have a grueling effect. The dirt gets stuck, especially in those horn parts with less density, less resistance and more moisture content. That's exactly the part where inner hoof wall tubules meet the epidermal lamellae. The dirt and possibly pathogens work their way deeper and deeper straight up, vertically into the hoof.

On the right side, we have different forces destroying the hoof capsule; tensile forces. They work laterally, to the side. The hoof wall is being pulled away from the center, so it is not under the load and has lost its bearing function. The quarter wall starts to bend. The tubules flare, chip and start pulling on the lamellar layer. The complete suspensory apparatus is out of balance. The lamellae stretch because they have no other choice. The dermal lamellae react with the release of hemoglobin as a sign of stress. Even the horn of the white line, the terminal horn, is affected. The connection is still given, just stretched. Dirt cannot stick on that side because it would be pushed to the side, not upward. However, bacteria can stick. They find their way into the stressed elongated lamellae.

The x-ray (different horse) shows the problem perfectly.

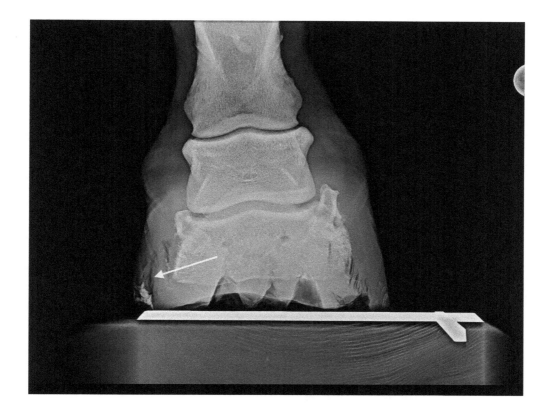

The arrow points to the cavity. The translucent part shows the gap. The hoof is mainly loaded on that lateral side (left in the picture). The whole bone column has shaped accordingly. The hoof wants to shape like that as well, but it can't. The more loaded side is bent. It is compressed. In the first third of that quarter wall is a kink. The hoof wall tries to grow out in a different, steeper angulation than below that kink. The hoof wall on that side has gained too much length. The hoof trimmer tried to adjust, 'balancing' the other, crooked looking and longer hoof side by cutting it down and making it shorter (right in the picture). Unfortunately, the bones will not follow that attempt of correction. They can't. The more loaded lateral quarter wall won't either. It will then become longer. More horn length at that one-sided overloaded hoof wall will result in separation because it cannot flare. The hoof wall can't bend as much as it does on the other side, where the forces can work to the side. Due to that, shear forces will cause a separation on the more loaded side. That's why those cavities are found exclusively on the more loaded parts of the hoof.

The situation is different when the lamellar layer and the white line itself are affected:

The arrow on the right side in the picture points to a torn lamellar layer, decomposed with bacteria, which have also eaten their way deep into the inside of the hoof. The left arrow marks a cavity. Horn separation can be seen on the more stressed side. Both problems can occur at the same time in one hoof or separately. Anything is possible. It depends on the individual hoof deformation. It is important to differentiate and to understand the causes so that the correct hoof treatment can take place.

The examples on the next page show how the white line or lamellar layer can be affected all around. Note that the most affected areas are exactly located where the hoof wall causes the most tensile forces. Soaking the hoof with anti-fungal or any kind of hoof treatment would make no sense at all. The affected areas will grow out when the hoof shape is being corrected. The stretched lamellae will grow down in a closed unit.

The bacteria can also affect the hoof wall, sometimes in combination with the lamellar layer.

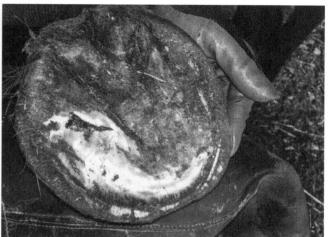

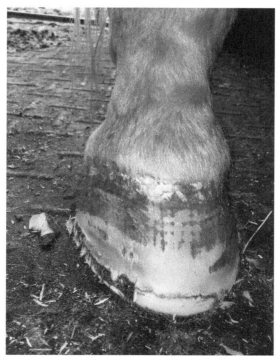

The cause is the same (leverage), making it possible for the bacteria to invade the horn.

In this case below, the hoof wall was separated all around from its lamellar layer in both fore feet:

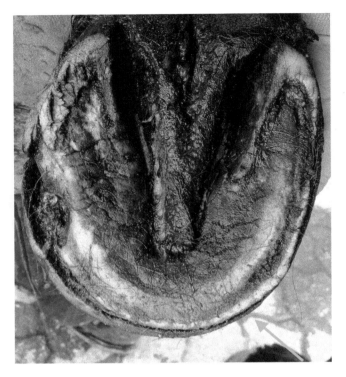

After 5 months:

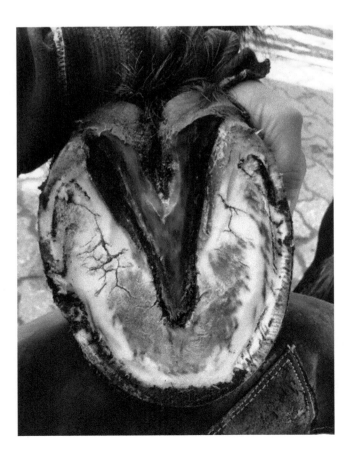

Improving the hoof shape improved the overall condition.

The next case is a left hind foot:

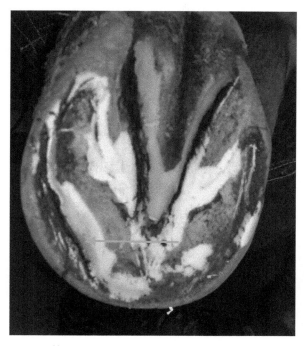

Behind the lateral quarter wall was a deep cavity. The wall was completely separated from the sole. The main load was on that lateral heel (left in the picture). From the dorsal view, we see a bent medial hoof wall (left in picture), a flare.

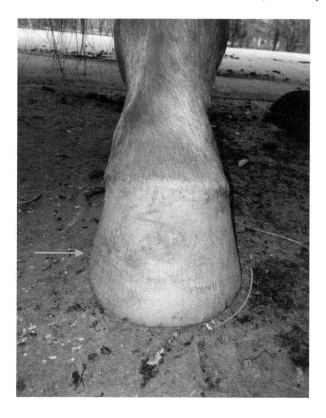

The arrow points to horizontal stress lines, horn tubules that are compressed and fold. The red curve marks the area where the hoof wall is unphysiologically rounded. The quarter wall on that side looks flared too, but actually it isn't. The physical forces happening on that side are not comparable to a flare. The opposite is the case. The quarter wall on that side is thick and strong. Compression forces are acting on that side. Due to an arthritis problem in his left hock, the horse changed its walking pattern in that limb. He sort of twists the hoof while in motion. The hoof wall on that side rounds unphysiologically, creating a very stiff, strong foundation and slowly separating from its center. It doesn't always have to be flare that creates leverage. The horse has had that separation for years. If the hoof shape doesn't change and the forces are not controlled, the gap will never disappear.

Only 1 month later:

The gap is slowly closing. Flushing it with copper sulfate helps to eliminate pathogens. I packed it with bee's wax, which helps prevent new dirt from getting into the gap.

Another month later:

4 months later:

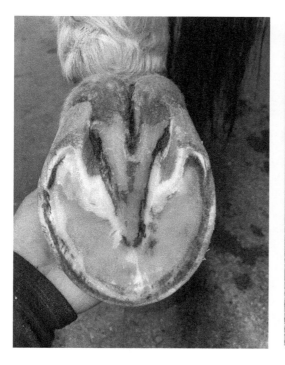

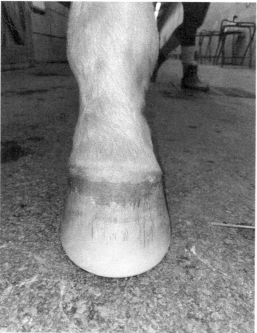

Chapter 4:
Before and After Pictures

The last chapter will show comparison pictures before the first treatment and after rehabilitation. The time between the results varies from half a year to 1.5 years. I did not add any comments on purpose so that you could yourself inspect the signs of distortion and evaluate the hooves yourself, now with more-educated eyes after what you have learned in this book.

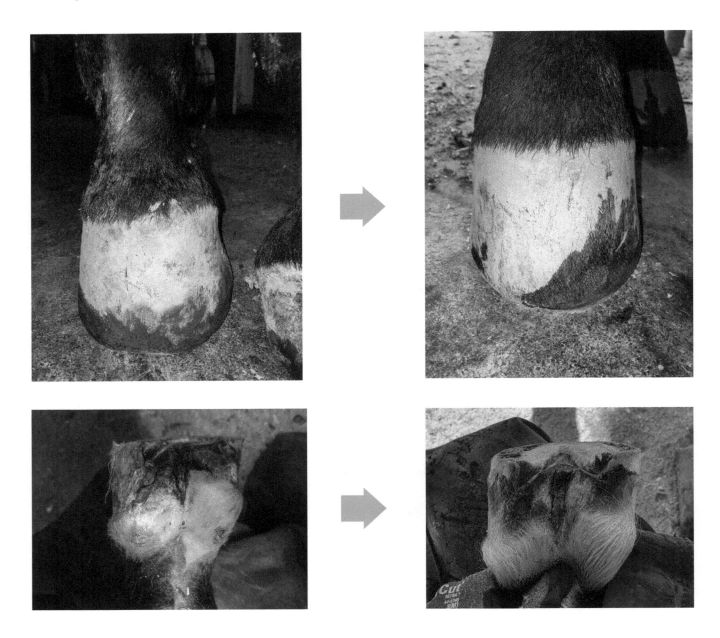

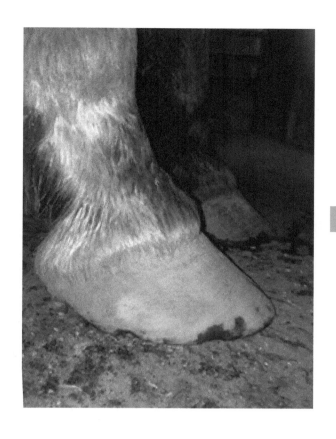
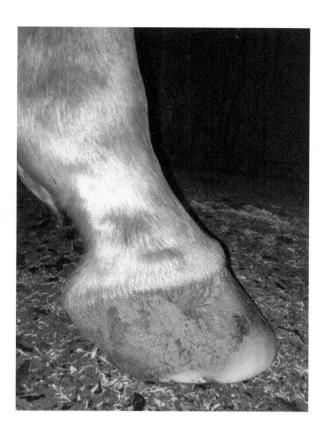
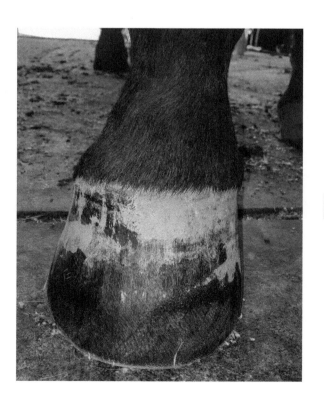

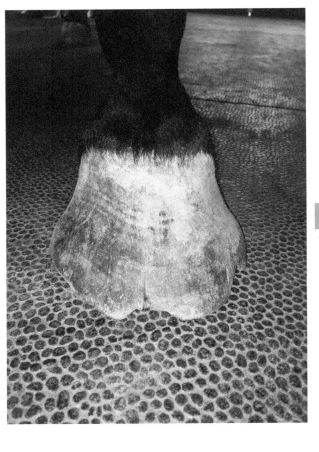 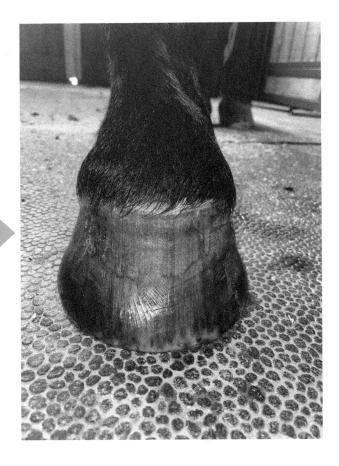

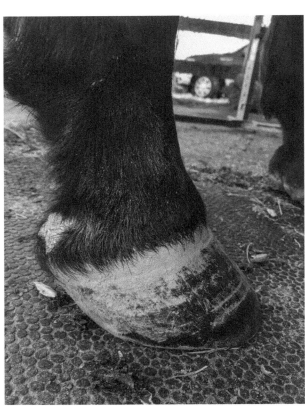 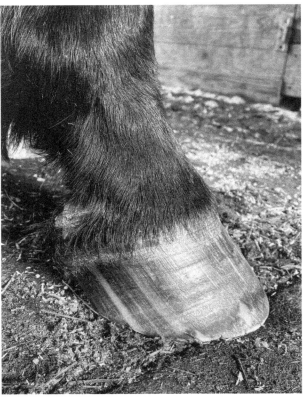

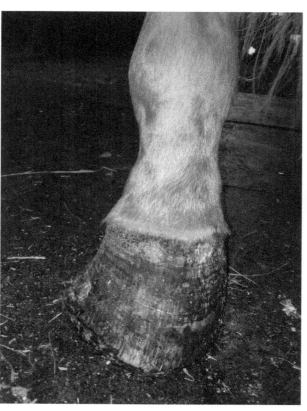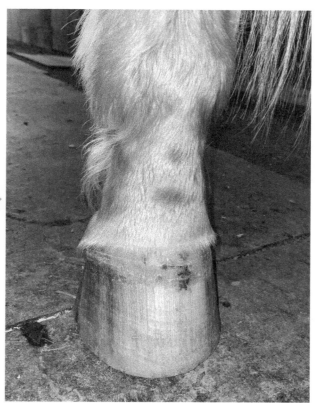

 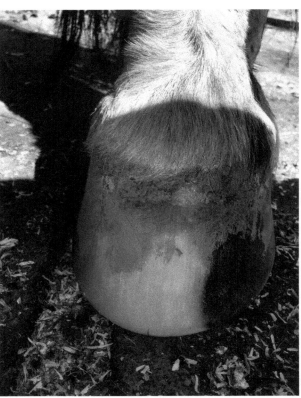

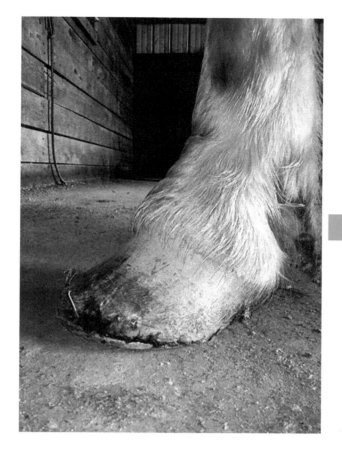 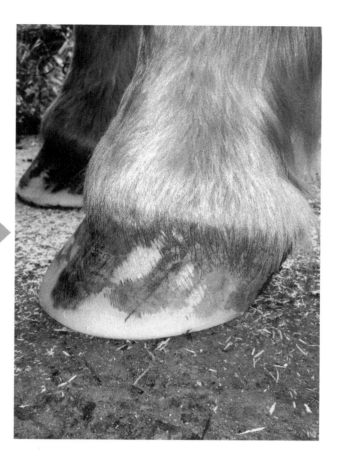

Basic Anatomy Used in this Book

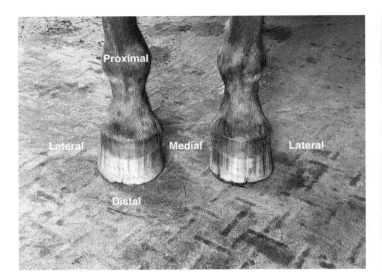

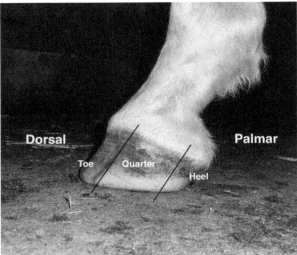

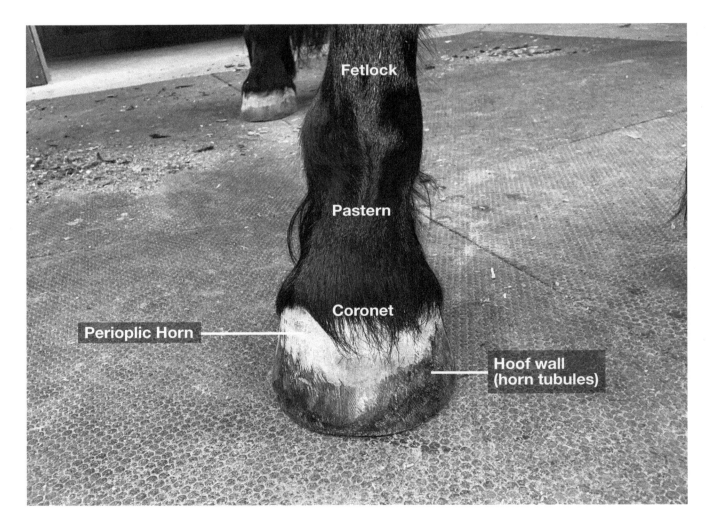

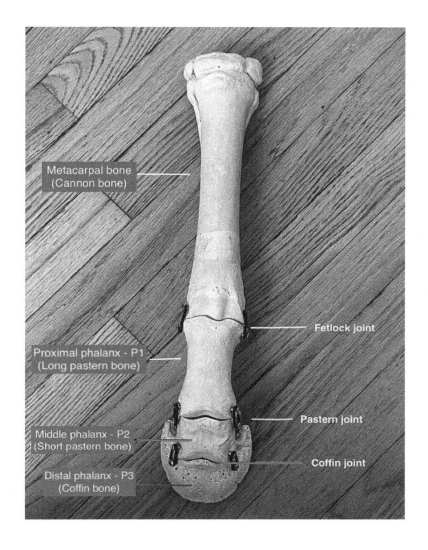

Metacarpal bone
(Cannon bone)

Fetlock joint

Proximal phalanx - P1
(Long pastern bone)

Pastern joint

Middle phalanx - P2
(Short pastern bone)

Coffin joint

Distal phalanx - P3
(Coffin bone)

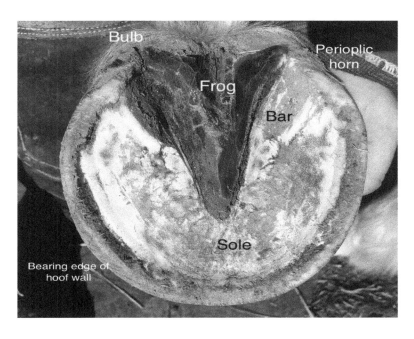

Bulb

Perioplic
horn

Frog

Bar

Sole

Bearing edge of
hoof wall

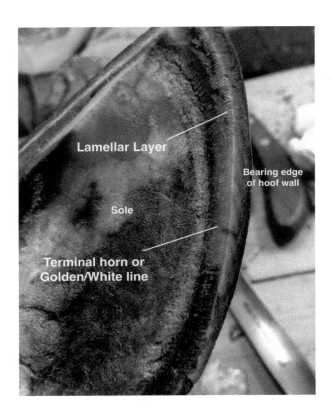

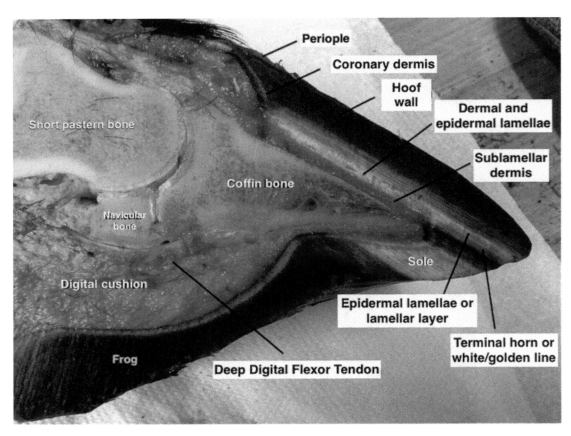

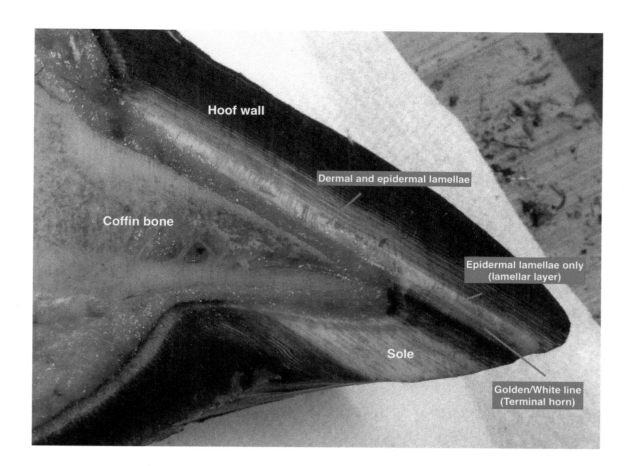

Hoof wall

Dermal and epidermal lamellae

Coffin bone

Epidermal lamellae only (lamellar layer)

Sole

Golden/White line (Terminal horn)

Perioplic horn

Tubules of hoof wall

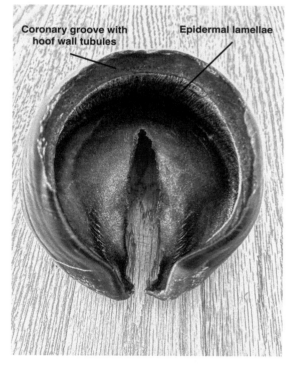

Coronary groove with hoof wall tubules

Epidermal lamellae

Epilogue

Dear horse owner, I would like to thank you for the time you have invested in this book.

I wrote it with the motivation of spreading this wonderful methodology. Like many of my hoof colleagues, I was dissatisfied with my horse's hoof conditions and with the existing approaches that were not getting me anywhere.

What started as a hobby became a vocation calling, a passion that won't let me go.

I hope I could infect you a little bit with this passion. If I can help only one horse, the effort was worth it. My goal is to reach as many people as possible who are also looking for answers to their hoof problems. I can guarantee that with this methodology, you will find the solution. I would like to educate and inspire you with this alternative approach. In the 21st century, we no longer have to compromise and accept the old ways that noticeably do not work.

If we want healthy horses in the long run, we must address the real cause of a problem instead of sticking a Band-Aid on the current symptom. The fast and comfortable way is not always the better way. In the long run, the right way saves a lot of grief, time and money, and provides you with the answers you were looking for.

The Center for Hoof Physics is at your disposal for questions about your horse's hoof problems. For the evaluation of hooves, consultations and information about the education, please visit **www.hoofphysics.com**

CPSIA information can be obtained
at www.ICGtesting.com
Printed in the USA
LVHW071522290422
717450LV00016BA/180

9 781088 020326